VOICES OF THE ANCIENTS

STEPHEN B. SHAFFER

VOICES OF THE ANCIENTS

STEPHEN B. SHAFFER

COUNCIL PRESS
AN IMPRINT OF CEDAR FORT, INC.
SPRINGVILLE, UTAH

ISBN 13: 978-1-4621-1022-3

Published by Council Press, an imprint of Cedar Fort, Inc.
2373 W. 700 S., Springville, UT 84663
Distributed by Cedar Fort, Inc., www.cedarfort.com

LIBRARY OF CONGRESS CATALOGING-IN-PUBLICATION DATA

Shaffer, Stephen B., author.
Voices of the ancients / S. B. Shaffer.
pages cm
Includes bibliographical references.
Summary: Discusses the ancient people who inhabited North America before Book of Mormon times.
ISBN 978-1-4621-1022-3
1. Paleo-Indians--North America--History. 2. Indians of North America--Antiquities. 3. Utah--Antiquities. 4. Michigan--Antiquities. 5. Archaeology--Utah. 6. Archaeology--Michigan. I. Title.

E61.S53 2012
970.004'97--dc23

2012001987

Cover design by Brian Halley

Edited and typeset by Emily S. Chambers

Printed in the United States of America

10 9 8 7 6 5 4 3 2 1

I DEDICATE THIS BOOK TO ALL THOSE WHO SHARE WITH ME THE DESIRE TO LEARN AND EXPAND THEIR KNOWLEDGE IN HISTORICAL EVENTS OF OUR PAST.

Also by Stephen Shaffer

Treasures of the Ancients

Out of the Dust: Utah's Lost Mines and Treasures

CONTENTS

CHAPTER 1
FOOTPRINTS

The expanse of America staggers the imagination when one views the splendorous beauty of its mountains, deserts, and valleys. The landscape has changed much since the days of Adam when land masses were thought to be solid, animals were more plentiful, and water covered great portions of it. With a good imagination a person can stand at the base of the Rocky Mountains and see the ghosts of the past while bathing in the beauty of those grand monarchs of granite and limestone.

The diversity of America's landscapes must have enthralled the ancient traveler as he wandered throughout the land. Man came into this vast wilderness to search out everything from freedom and food, to minerals, mates, slaves, and commerce.

While no one disputes that the Americas were first peopled by groups from Asia, Africa, and Europe many thousands of years ago, what is not known exactly is how they got here. It is believed by many that the first people to come to America arrived by crossing a land bridge that once connected Siberia with North America. Others suppose that the first inhabitants came from beyond the stars in spacecrafts of a curious design. Still others presume that America's first people came by ship across the Pacific Ocean. Let's take a closer look at each of these theories about how North America might have first become populated.

Theories of Early North American Inhabitants

The first theory, and possibly the most popular, is one being taught in virtually every school in the United States and suggests that people came from Siberia across a land bridge. Professor of Anthropology, John McDonough, teaching at a Kennedy University told his students that

> There were perhaps two dozen in the band of fur clad hunters. They camped in the Siberian tundra in a small cluster of tents fashioned of caribou fur and wood. Inside the tents the ground had been dug out a foot or so below the surface to help protect the hunters from the bitterly cold Arctic wind. Soon it would be time to break camp and move on. The herds of caribou, bison, and horses, whose carcasses gave the hunters food and clothing and the materials for shelter, were migrating once again. The hunters must gather up their weapons, fold their tents, and follow the animals—or perish.

The Professor claimed that during this migration, about 18,000 years ago, glaciers penetrated deep into the Northern Hemisphere and locked up so much of the world's ocean water that the overall sea level was some 400 feet lower than it is now. The sites of today's coastal cities, such as New York, were well inland and the lowered sea level exposed a 1,000-mile-wide land bridge—which has been dubbed "Beringia"—connecting Alaska and Siberia. According to some, it was across Beringia, which vanished and reappeared with the ebb and flow of the glaciers, that the first immigrants to America came. Their goal was neither to explore nor to settle, but merely to pursue the migrating animal herds—such as caribou—for food. Professor McDonough's description provides great detail of the hunters' pursuit and of their everyday dealings, making for a wonderful and colorful story. Without a shred of evidence to support the theory, this is what it remains—simply a story. Anyone with knowledge of that forbidding land northward will understand that such a theory is full of many holes.

Several years ago, in an attempt to prove the Beringia land bridge theory, a convoy of Russian explorers and scientists decided to see if it were possible to make the trek from central Siberia to the Bering Sea. They, unlike their predecessors, determined to use more conventional means for their journey. They enlisted the aid of several tundra vehicles, modern cooking stoves, gasoline, tents, mummy bags, freeze-dried foods, and modern sub-zero clothing—providing them with all the comforts of home. Despite the attempt, the Russians never made it to their destination. The Siberian summer was like a northern Minnesota winter. Their mummy bags did not keep them warm. Their food ran out. There was no game to hunt. They called for assistance and left that forsaken wilderness assured that an ancient people, dressed in skins and more than likely on foot, could not have survived to make it to the Bering Sea. As for evidence of mammals, such as caribou, horses, and ox, they found nothing. It is doubtful that the tundra in Siberia could have supported wildlife in the numbers that Professor McDonough suggested since only certain animals can survive on tundra grasses. Further, the idea of walking across a frozen wasteland at a distance greater than from the U.S.-Canadian border to central Mexico is also rather hard to believe. Additionally, there is no way the travelers could have carried enough fuel with them to keep a fire going. Even if there happened to be hordes of animals, and if the travelers used their droppings, they still would not have had enough fuel.

The second theory about how the Americas may have been first populated comes from the idea that we came into existence by aliens from another planet—that we are descendants of space travelers.

On a sheer sandstone wall in southern Utah, a ghostly figure stands out against the desert sun (Figure 1.1). It appears to have antennas sticking out of its head, and has the appearance of a man in a space suit. Some people have presumed that the Indians[1] of the region carved the figure on the wall to depict their ancestral heritage. These ancient Americans believed that they were left to struggle through life, to learn by their mistakes. Their outer-world ancestors left them in a state of ignorance without knowledge of their other life or those who brought them to this world. One Hopi Elder has said that these space travelers were banished from the skies. Such ideas are not to be scoffed at. Some of the American Indians believe this theory as much as you or I believe our own theories about how we came to be here. They believe a lone sandstone mound located in a remote canyon in southeastern Utah further supports the theory of extraterrestrial ancestry. The mound, situated on the western edge of the White Mountain Ute Reservation, is nestled at the end of a larger mountainous arm and sided by two small streams. The mound is approximately two hundred feet long and fifty feet high at its center. When approaching the mound from the south it is easy to see. A dirt road runs directly south of it, and at one time a small meadow between the road and the mound was farmed by a homesteader. To access the property, one must drive to the eastern edge of the mound, then hike up the east face, or trespass to the south face. The south face is where the most important clues can be found as to its origin.

Some years ago, I had the opportunity to investigate this site, when I was contacted by a pair of brothers interested in learning more about its beginnings. We met at Blanding, Utah the night before our trek to the site to discuss our plan for the next morning. The two informed me that the White Mountain Utes would be watching the area, so we would have to be careful where we went. They told me that the site was on private property, but had since been abandoned. The east side of the mound was located on Ute tribal property as was the side canyon to the east. The brothers went on to tell me that when they attempted to access this side canyon for the purpose of further investigating the mound, they were met by angry Ute's who informed them they were trespassing and must leave immediately.

We began the trip by driving from Blanding toward Hanksville, got off the main highway on Cottonwood Canyon Road and headed north. Some miles further in, we finally came to the mound site. At first glance, the area looked to me like a thousand other abandoned homestead sites across the Southwest. We got out of our vehicles and crossed the fence at the east side of the property. The two brothers took me to the south side of the mound where they parted the thick brush to reveal a panel with some very strange rock ideograms,[2] petroglyphs,[3] and hieroglyphs.[4]

Upon inspecting the panel I was surprised by what I saw. The two men pointed out a clear and distinct outline of a mountain range. A sun protruded from behind the mountains on the right side of the panel. Three drill holes were detected and two obvious symbols indicating distance and an opening were clearly displayed. More important, at the center of the panel was a strange symbol, which appeared to be a five-sided star with the manifestation of upward movement set in a mountain valley (Figure 1.2). The "star" had five angled lines coming off each one of its horizontal arms. Inside of the star I could see several more horizontal and angled lines and an "X" and "+" sign. The "movement upward" sign appeared at the bottom of the star. Other lines off the tips of the star indicated its location in regards to the surrounding mountains.

As I examined the figures, I noted that the sun had special features as well and I could see that it was a rising sun and exhibited twelve rays (Figure 1.3). This in itself is an important feature. The drill holes in this panel may depict cave entrances or important geological points of interests, but inserting small sticks in the holes proved fruitless as there could be no shadow thrown at that site.

At the far left of this panel is found a small diamond shape with a dot in its center. At the far lower right, near a drill hole, is found the mark usually intended to indicate "tunnel, cave, or dwelling," or in this case because of the horizontal lines in its face, possibly a "mound."

The most important panel of the sandstone mound, in my opinion, are two stone teepees found a short distance from the above-mentioned panel (Figure 1.4). The two teepees are filled with signs and symbols. But even more significant is the presence of what appears to be a spacecraft or crafts launching from between these two teepees and ascending to symbols of a thunderbird and a star overhead. At the sides of the teepees appear letters or symbols associated with this mound site only. Rays appear from each teepee. At first glance, these appear to be lodge poles but then after counting the lines it seems they represent something different than common poles used in erecting a teepee. The teepees themselves are constructed from what appears to be stone. The entrances are covered and have diagrams or symbols cut into them. Other symbols adorn the skin of the teepees.

Moving eastward we found another very important feature. On the face of the mound is depicted what appears to be an alien form, as so commonly portrayed in today's pop culture and in star travel publications (Figure 1.5).

The top of the mound is covered with geo-glyphs, petroglyphs, and ideograms. Our first attempt to photograph all of these signs was hampered by snow and ice on top of the mound. Another attempt was made the following summer when all the signs were noted and logged. To my surprise we even found some panels that had not been previously discovered by the two brothers. One such panel includes a very large spider petroglyph (Figure 1.6) located on the eastern side of the rock mound that measures five feet by three feet.

Figure 1.7 is very interesting simply because of the sun cross that seems to be attached to the beak of a fancy carved bird. We have little information on the meaning of the bird but I feel it may represent a map of sorts. This particular sun cross can be traced to similar-looking sun crosses used as the symbol of divine victory of the sun on the earliest Sumerian (or Early Aryan) sacred seals from about 4000 BC. These sun crosses are also used by the Hittites, Kassis, Trojans, Phoenicians, Goths, and Ancient Britons, and worn as an amulet down through the ages into the Christian era. The sun cross has been figured both in the simple form, and also decorated and ornamented in various ways like a jewel. There are over 150 different renditions of the sun cross.

Figures 1.8 and 1.9 reflect two more carved cross symbols found at the site. Figure 1.8 is recognized as the "Malta" or "Maltese" symbol. It is said that this cross was used to signify victory by some explorers. This cross is not a sign of the Christian cross because it was used much earlier than Christ's crucifixion. Some time after Christ's death (circa AD 340) the Goths introduced the Victory Cross as a sun cross, but it was not a substitute for the crucifix. Not until the tenth century was Christ represented to the public on the true cross as a crucifix, and impaled thereon, blood-splashed, in agony and death, in the form now familiar. The question then here is: What is the meaning of this particular sun cross? and more important, Who put it there? We can only make educated guesses and do more research to finally discover the answers.

The entire mound and its glyphs raise the question as to who it was that inscribed them (Figure 1.10). To look at these inscriptions, one might wonder if they are simply the work of modern-day pranksters. But upon closer examination there are little, subtle inscriptions that, due to their placement, could not have been forged. Only someone with knowledge of symbols of various forms could have placed them as they appear (Figure 1.11). It makes one wonder if this mound was used by extraterrestrials as a landing site, or perhaps the glyphs could have been carved by an old Ute sage, whose night visions told him of a future time when such things would be commonplace.

Another theory that has surfaced in the past few years about who may have created the site is that of the Mawshak Moors. It is believed that these ancient Africans migrated from areas known as Kush, Ethiopia, Uganda, Somalia, and Sudan and were the original mound-builders. The theory claims that these

Africans came to this continent thousands of years ago, bringing with them an advanced pyramid-mound-building knowledge, along with advanced sciences, mathematics, and astronomy. This mound-building culture is well-known among the Etowah Moors of Western Africa who built the ancient Etowah mounds—the largest of these mounds standing sixty-three feet above the sandy loam of the Etowah River Valley. The Etowah Moors successfully farmed beans, corn, and squash—known as the "Three Sisters"—in the Etowah River Valley. It was this that gave these mound-builders the ability to forsake the hunter society for an agricultural one. It is said that the villages of the mound-builders were larger than any European village, and much more advanced agriculturally.

But historians also claim that Africans could not have discovered America thousands of years ago because they did not know how to build ships to face the harsh Atlantic Ocean. It is more probable that the Africans of that area were used as slaves aboard sea-worthy ships that were built by the Libyans or Phoenicians.

Whatever the origin of the sandstone mound in Cottonwood Canyon, I believe there is much more to this site than first meets the eye, and that it was most likely a canvas for several different artists. Unlocking the mystery of this Utah mound is an intriguing prospect, which I hope may someday be realized. My interpretation and investigation of the site and all of its fascinating symbols is an ongoing project. It may take several years to make any sense of this site, but with the help of the many societies dedicated to this type of work and commitment to finding the truth concerning historical sites such as this, we plan to come to a satisfactory conclusion.

NOTES

1. The term used by mainstream academia, "Native American" in reference to the American Indian only, is an insult to every

American born citizen including the American Indian who has tribal identities and personalities differing from one tribe to another. I prefer referring to my American Indian brothers and sisters by their tribal affiliation.

2. *Ideogram:* a symbol that expresses an idea or concept understandable to all people, regardless of differences in language; an idea expressed in a symbol containing no phonetic elements.
3. *Petroglyph:* symbols made on rock by pecking, incising, abrading, or scratching.
4. *Hieroglyph:* true picture writing, with agreement between the picture and its meaning.

CHAPTER II
LOST CIVILIZATIONS

We have been taught in public schools that not more than a handful of explorers ever set foot on American soil. We have textbooks and maps that imply the American continent was inhabited by peoples whose ancestors crossed a land bridge from Asia to this continent tens of thousands of years ago. We are taught that no European, Asian, African or any other peoples except for a few lost Vikings ever came to North America. Columbus is given credit for "discovering" America and we still celebrate this discovery even though many scholars and historians are beginning to become disenchanted by this over-rated event.

New evidence is constantly emerging suggesting that this continent was indeed inhabited by many different races and cultures. Early archeological evidence by carbon dating show remains of an archaic maritime "Red Paint People" living in Labrador and New England as far back as 5000 BC, with evidence of sea-worthy wooden vessels of similar design on both sides of the Atlantic.

Around 4000 BC there appeared dolmens[1] in the British Isles and Europe. Such dolmens have also appeared on the shores of North America dated very near that same timeline, which we will explore further in a later chapter.

One of the most compelling discoveries suggesting New World exploration by an ancient sea-faring people is what is known as the "Old Copper culture" of northern Michigan and Lake Superior. Ancient tools and other artifacts have been carbon dated to circa 2000 BC with over 5000 copper mines being in operation near Copper Peninsula dating to that same period. It has been estimated, by reputable mining engineers, that millions of pounds of copper were extracted from these mines and exported abroad by the Old Copper culture.[2]

According to mining researcher C. Fred Rydholm, around 1700 BC, Nordic navigator-traders came to Ontario from Scandinavia, bringing woven textiles as trade material for Canadian copper ingots,[3] and then shipped the ingots back to Scandinavia. To support the claim is a pictorial record annotated in Tifinag script—an early Norse language—reporting their religious, astronomical, calendaring, and trading interests, in their contacts with the Algonquians.[4]

In addition, many Celtiberian and Ogham[5] inscriptions have been found carved on bone and on stone artifacts both above ground and in ancient graves throughout the Midwestern United States that carbon date to circa 250 BC.

The non-stop migration of European and African cultures continued right up through AD 1492 when Columbus sailed with Basque pilots to the islands of the Caribbean.

Some scholars believe that ancient explorers kept east of the Mississippi River, but this is not so. Much evidence has been uncovered suggesting there were perhaps dozens of different races and cultures that came into the Rocky Mountains for one reason or another. Perhaps they came for the same reason the Spanish conquistadors came: to look for mineral wealth! Perhaps it was for medicinal plants or strange and exotic animals that they could transport back to their homelands. Or perhaps they needed slaves to man their mighty vessels. Whatever the reasons were, we do know they came.

It is reasonable to believe that finding Egyptian hieroglyphs in North America is not plausible. However, there are twenty-nine known sites in the western United States where strange Egyptian-type hieroglyphs have been discovered! As these fantastic panels became known and visited over the years, many professionals from archaeologists to Egyptologists began publishing their findings and theories surrounding these strange hieroglyphs. No two professionals came up with the same idea as to origin or transliteration.

There have been six sites documented of this type of hieroglyphic writing in Utah, while a seventh site above Brigham Young University in Provo, Utah has been proved to be a fake—carved by a group of students in the 1930s.[6] I have decided to write about these documented sites in Utah since they have other historical significance besides the inscriptions themselves.

It is now accepted by most scholars that the Spanish came into Utah in search of mineral wealth long before the Dominquez/Escalate Expedition came in 1776. Rumors abounded among the Spanish explorers in South America that there was so much gold and silver in the "Yuta" country that it was easy to obtain. Of course we know this wasn't the case, but it prompted expedition leaders to make their way north in search of these riches.

It is with some certainty that these Spaniards were made aware of the possibility of riches cached by an earlier people—other than the native Indians they encountered—that inhabited the West. There are stories and legends about the Spanish plundering tombs of ancient races along their route through Arizona and Utah. Spanish armor has been discovered in and around the hieroglyph sites in Utah over the years. Interviews, which I conducted with Ute Indians of Eastern Utah, revealed knowledge of an ancient race of giants that inhabited the land at one time. They spoke a strange language and came from the west. The strange hieroglyphs were thought to have been carved by these ancient people. Others have alluded to the idea that these inscriptions are the work of a race of people that came from Jerusalem around 600 BC and flourished in North America until their demise in circa AD 400. According to this theory, they are thought to be the ancestors of the American Indian of today.

In the 1960s, one explorer by the name of Jose Davila, spent an enormous amount of time and money trying to prove that the site of one great panel in a canyon east of Fillmore, Utah was in fact inscribed by this ancient people from Jerusalem, also known as the Nephites. Davila was so certain that the site was that of an ancient Nephite treasure that his sole purpose became to find and extract this treasure trove! He even went as far as to translate the panel using recourses such as Wallis Budges' *An Egyptian Hieroglyphic Dictionary*, Barry Fell's *Polynesian Discovery of America*, and Alan Gardiner's *Egyptian Grammar*. Little did Davila know that using these references would not give him a full understanding of the inscriptions but only cause him to become more driven to find the treasure. This drive would ultimately cause the deaths of two young men hired to dig for the cache![7]

After the Davila saga, many more scholars would attempt their hand at deciphering the panel at Fillmore as well as the other panels in Utah and surrounding states. It seemed that none came to a collective conclusion as to the origin or translation of the glyphs.

Curiosity in the Utah hieroglyphic panels waned for some time until a renewed interest came about when a Spanish sword was discovered in a canyon east of Fillmore, Utah, and a strange carved man, commonly referred to as "The Shot Put Man" (see Figure 2.1) was found on a large flat rock near Cedar City, Utah close to another panel very similar to that of the one in Fillmore. Still other panels in Utah, such as those near Manti, Nephi, Ogden, and Lake Powell, stirred new interest when it was discovered that these sites had something in common: their elevation. Other exciting discoveries caused excitement when glyphs of rock turtles and dragons, and large rock cairns with inscriptions, were discovered in these same locations.

At one time, inscriptions of a dragon and turtle sat above The Shot Put Man high on a ridgeline, but either time or vandals have destroyed these valuable landmarks. An eye symbol and a perpendicular line give searchers direction to a hidden panel of hieroglyphs, also near Cedar City (Figure 2.2). Unfortunately some of the inscriptions have been vandalized and even removed from their age-old home by some thoughtless, uncaring person or group with no regard to their historical significances!

Nestled behind a temple owned and operated by the Church of Jesus Christ of Latter-day Saints in Manti, Utah is an old rock quarry where stones for the temple were removed for its construction. During this period (1875-76) a panel of strange inscriptions (Figure 2.3) was discovered that matches those of all the others discovered in the West. There are some slight differences between all the panels in terms of the arrangement of the inscriptions, but for the most part, all the panels are similar. The Manti panel seemed to appear much older than the others and was passed by countless times due to a heavy layer of lichen that hid it from view. Across the quarry to the north there are more inscriptions of the same type but a little larger in appearance (Figure 2.4). Near this site and up on top of a butte there appears to be the foundation of an ancient building of some type.

Appearing on the north side of the quarry there is evidence that, long ago, a large structure once stood. The evidence left there indicates that large rectangle slabs of stone were quarried and dragged to this location as a floor for this large building. Strange cup-shaped holes are found at the southern end of where the structure once stood. Near the west side and close to the center is found a circular pit that may have been used as a bathing place or baptismal font; strange placement of boulders along the western side reveal that at one time a place of entrance was there.

A little farther north, in the town of Ephraim, Utah is a rounded, man-made hill commonly known as "Witches Knoll" by locals (Figure 2.5). Ground-penetrating radar conducted by Earthview of Salt Lake City, Utah reveals a buried structure under the mound with walls and rooms. It is very evident that this mound covers a dwelling of sorts and was known as a sacred place by the local Ute population before the arrival of the Mormon settlers in the mid 1800s. It has been linked to the Manti site as well as a host of other strange anomalies throughout Sanpete Valley, Utah.

The Fillmore Panel or Chalk Creek Panel

The Fillmore Panel, which Jose Davila spent so much time trying to prove was part of an ancient Nephite site, is important in light of its connection to the rest of the Utah panels. Much has been written concerning this panel, but continuing research has proven this site much more valuable than first thought.

In one of my previous books, I include excerpts from a 1982 interview, conducted by Tom Stinson, Bill Wright, and Darlene Mundy of the Fillmore Ranger District Office, with Clifford Purcell, an aging Fillmore prospector who gave fascinating details about his discovery of the Fillmore Panel in the late 1930s:

> Looking for copper, silver or iron ore in 1939, Clifford Purcell and his companion, Rube Melville, a Fillmore café owner, were searching the slopes above Chalk Creek when Purcell noticed the hieroglyphics. He stated that "there is four rows kinda like picture writing . . . full of lichen, full of green stuff . . . The sun was shining on it like a spotlight. The lichen almost filled the grooves . . . I'll tell you about a man who may know something about this . . . .[The] man Frank Beckwith from Delta . . . .I got Frank Beckwith to go look at it . . . He took pictures and everything. He determined that the writings dated the earliest settlers by 500 to 600 years. Then we marked the writings with chalk and took pictures of them."[8]

In the interview Purcell also talked about "Signature Rock," which is now on display behind the Fillmore District Office. When it was in place it was positioned just north of the Fillmore panel some several feet. It was around 1965 when treasure-hunter Davila and a local by the name of Del Allgood were working the site and somehow dislodged the rock, causing it to tumble down and come to rest below the main panel. Consequently it was gathered up and taken to the district office.

It was during this time; 1939, that Purcell and Melville mentioned that they also knew where a "map rock" was located that was full of the same color and type of lichen[9] (Figure 2.6).

It was thought that a cache might rest beneath the large rock where the map was carved, but with a little probing it was decided there was no cache at that site. The map rock was more or less left alone but visited often by curious folks thinking they might figure out its meaning.

Many years passed; Davila had left the mountains, and the thrill of possibly finding a lost treasure hidden somewhere in the region east of Fillmore had dwindled. But in 1990, a spark of renewed interest in the site once again flared up when I was contacted by a young woman from Sanpete County with an incredible story to tell me! The young woman, "Kate" (I will call her as she asked me to keep her identity anonymous) told me of a man that worked for her and her husband doing odd jobs around their trailer park. He relayed a story about a lost cache of gold hidden somewhere high in the mountains east of Fillmore that had been discovered by two cowboys around 1972 who were pushing their cattle out of the high country before the winter snows came. As Kate told the man's story, my thoughts drifted back to another incident I knew of related to this supposed cache, where an Idaho rancher and amateur treasure-hunter named Sam Holbrook, and his friends, traveled from Idaho and California to hunt for it:

Holbrook's interest in the cache began when a childhood friend told him about a Utah mining venture where he and his brother had stumbled upon a rock with strange symbols on it. The friend gave Holbrook a postcard with the writings on it, which captured his imagination and started an obsession for Holbrook that would last for almost two decades.

The legends surrounding the ancient writings on the rock are many and varied. One story involves a navigator for Cortez and his lover who had buried the treasure when they ran into trouble with the Indians of the area and had marked the place so they could come back later and retrieve it. Another tale claims that Father Escalante's expeditions through the area were attempts to find this vast horde. Whatever the origins of the inscriptions on the rock, Holbrook remained transfixed by them and carried the postcard with the rock's markings with him always.

In the early 1960s, Holbrook continued to do research on the symbols, showing the postcard to an acquaintance with a knowledge of ancient languages who stated that he believed the symbols to be ancient Crete or possibly Phoenician, with a symbol or two of Aztec.

It wasn't until the autumn of 1974 that Holbrook had a chance to actually act on his desire to come down from Idaho and search for the treasure in Fillmore. Holbrook notes in his journal,[9] "After climbing and crawling up hills and down, th[r]ough brush and rocks, I was on a deer trail heading [back] and skidded down a bank and there it was—symbols and all just as Jim had described it to me. Quite a feeling of elation, awe, and wonder all in one." He then describes in some detail that first attempt in 1974 of at least three where he tried to uncover the cache:

> As it was nearing dark [that day] . . . I noticed what seemed to be a large cave at the base of a cliff. It looked quite accessible from a distance but from the way it had to be reached it was darn hard to find . . . I came around a brushy point to a large rock slide and up this steep slide about a hundred yards was the cave I'd been looking for . . . The cave was approximately thirty feet deep as I remember it at this writing and maybe seven to eight feet wide at the entrance and possible eight feet high . . . The rock walls, ceiling, and the floor of the cave, as I recall, were quite hard and smooth surfaced, almost slick, while outside the slide and face of the cliff was coarse sandstone. Lying on the floor of the cave

> about a foot inside the entrance was a sandstone slab maybe two feet wide, four feet long and six inches thick. There was a space of maybe six inches, then a larger slab toward the back of the cave approximately the same size but about ten inches thick. Also lying on the floor were sand and pebbles that seemed to make everything blend together with a plumb natural appearance. I scraped the accumulation away with my foot . . . I did notice the roof of this cave above these rocks, and made a mental note that the slabs never came from the roof of the cave . . . I was getting a bit frantic—the sun was down, I was miles from camp, and I was physically done in . . . I did retain enough presence of mind, I hope, to make a mental note of my route in relation to the cave to be able to return . . . Now I can hardly wait for winter to pass and return with horses and tools to lead my friends to the cave and find what is under my two slabs of sandstone.

Sam Holbrook spent the winter of 1974-75 studying as much about archaeology pertaining to ancient Mediterranean areas, Mexico, and Central and South America as he could find. In June of 1975, Holbrook and his wife headed back to Utah to attempt to locate the treasure again. This time he took tools he thought he would need to remove the sandstone slabs he was sure were covering the treasure. He notes that "at first glance, upon entering the cave, I was quite bewildered. There was now two uniform slabs on a fairly smooth floor. The front of the cave looked different from inside as I remembered it." With the geographic changes to the cave, which Holbrook believed were possibly due to earthquakes or atomic testing in Nevada, he did not have the right tools or help to dislodge the slabs and his second attempt resulted in failure. Even though friends urged him to give up on the idea, Holbrook couldn't bring himself to do it: "I'm obsessed with this thing. My studies, knowledge of ancient history, religion, practices and beliefs will keep me going on this till I make at least another try. I'm going to recruit a couple or three tough, younger men and bust that big stone, shove out the dirt and get down to the two slabs and see what is underneath them."

Holbrook, along with a friend, made at least one, possibly two more tries at uncovering the treasure, but a wounded horse, bad weather, and again a cave that appeared to have changed since Holbrook's prior attempt thwarted his efforts. As he dreamed of returning again to the site the next year, he recorded the following: "The symbols are still on the rock and to me speak a message loud and clear for he who will translate and believe and persevere. But, god those hills are steep, rocky, and painful for one of my years. Can I make it again?"

Unfortunately, he never did. Holbrook died in 1979, never to return to Utah to look for his lost cave with the two slabs of sandstone.

With Sam Holbrook's attempts fresh in my mind and new information in hand from Kate, I became very interested in reviving the treasure hunt east of Fillmore, but more important, I wanted to prove that the Spanish did, in fact, mine gold in Utah before Escalante made his famous expedition through what is now Utah.

I needed to verify Kate's story with names and dates, so I contacted the very man who had told her the tale about the hidden cache found by the cowboys and asked him to tell me his story. I interviewed him several times and each time his story never varied. I was confident he was telling me the truth and that there was indeed a cache of gold bars hidden in the mountains near Fillmore, Utah!

In 2001 with renewed vigor I headed into the Fillmore hills to inspect the hieroglyphs and map rocks to see if there was something that had been missed by early researchers[11] and treasure hunters (or by me and my party as well). What I found were Spanish symbols deeply carved in very old trees and more important the names of the two cowboys! I knew we were on the right trail! Unfortunately, Utah has experienced some very bizarre weather over the years that have caused landslides and mudslides. In addition, trees that included some important markings have been killed by beetles. The landscape has changed drastically, but undaunted we continued our research!

NOTES

1. A *dolmen* is a table rock or memorial monument.
2. Rydholm, *Michigan Copper, The Untold Story*, 20-56.
3. An *ingot* is metal that is cast into a mold shape to make further processing easier.
4. *Algonquians* are an ancient race associated with the Adena Culture of Eastern North America circa. The Adena culture was a conglomerate of many different communities that inhabited the central and Southern regions of Ohio in the first millennium BC. The Adena people lived in villages and survived by hunting, fishing and gathering wild plants. Although the Adena culture survived for many centuries (500-100 BC), much of what we know of them today is drawn from mounds.
5. *Celtiberian* and *Ogaam*, or *Ogham*, are old world languages dating back to around 3000 BC (Gary Fell, *America B.C.*).
6. A Student At Brigham Young University admitted to having carved the hieroglyphs in the rock face near the "**Y**" in the mountain above Provo, Utah during his school years in the 1930s. His name is Earl Arnold and lives in Las Vegas, Nevada.
7. Shaffer, *Treasures of the Ancients*, 146-47.
8. Ibid., 151.
9. In archaeology, paleontology, and geomorphology, *lichenometry* is a geomorphic method of geochronology aging that uses lichen growth to determine the age of exposed rock: lichens are presumed to increase in size radically at specific rates as they grow. Measuring the diameter of the largest lichen of a species on a rock surface can therefore be used to determine the amount of time that the rock has been exposed. Lichen can be preserved on old rock faces for up to 10,000 years, providing the maximum age limit of the technique, though is most accurate (within 10 percent error) when applied to surfaces that have been exposed for less than 1000 years. The use of lichenometry is of increased value for dating deposited

surfaces over the past 500 years as radiocarbon dating techniques are less efficient over this period. The most common lichen used for lichenometry is that of the genus Rhizocarpon, for example the species Rhizocarpon geographicum, and those of the genus Xanthoria.

10. This narrative presented in the original spelling of Sam Holbrook. Supplied by the late Del Allgood of Fillmore, Utah.
11. Clifford Purcell and Rube Melville when chalking the Chalk Creek panel missed the grooves and cuts made by the original artists and even missed some hieroglyphs completely! The "Head" glyph was actually chalked closer to its original form than how it appears today.

CHAPTER iii
PATCHING HISTORY

I KNEW THERE HAD TO BE MORE TO THE FILLMORE PANEL THAN just the hieroglyphs and map rocks. I knew there had to be a reason the Spanish came to this site! It stands to reason they came for ancient treasure and I was almost certain they had discovered an ancient society and did to them what their predecessors had done to Montezuma. What the two cowboys had found were melted down treasures of the ancients that had been plundered by marauding Spanish conquistadors.

By using the "Blue Sky Nitch" sign (a symbol on the Fillmore panel), I decided to make the trek up and over the mountains east of Fillmore to where I could see such a place as was depicted. What I found was a very large and strange-looking mountain that resembled a step pyramid. This mountain is called Beehive Peak but I discovered from locals in the area that the peak had another name once used by the local Indians: "Pharaohs Peak"! This began to make sense to me so I knew there had to be more evidence and perhaps that evidence was near that large, odd-looking mountain.

Some months later I drove to a location east of Beehive Peak and began searching the area. To my amazement I discovered several strange-looking rock monuments that resembled a dozen or so similar structures at Fish Lake near Loa, Utah. I had always been told these particular rock monuments had been constructed by a bored sheepherder in the 1950s.

Relating my discovery to some of my colleagues, it was decided that since I was tied up at the time they would continue the search in the vast cedar forest east of Beehive for more monuments or other curious oddities. It wasn't long before we had counted over eighty rock monuments constructed in a curious manner and situated in strange lines and arrangements! The puzzle continued to grow and we became even more confused about the whole thing!

During this time I was contacted by an individual (who wishes to remain anonymous) who told me that someone had tried to steal the large map rock east of Fillmore. Not knowing what kind of damage had been done, I contacted Robert Leonard, an archeologist at the Forest Service Fish Lake District at Richfield, Utah and told him about the incident. He made the trip to Fillmore where it was discovered the large map rock had, indeed, been undermined and it appeared that someone had attempted to remove it! Because I had the GPS on its exact location and orientation before it was moved, Leonard asked for assistance in anchoring the rock. I was able to gather members of the We Nooch Society (an historical research and preservation society) to help in the restoration process. We were thankful the rock was not seriously damaged but dismayed to find that a smaller map rock nearby had been! We cemented and rocked in the main map rock and the Forest Service then placed large boulders around it to keep motor vehicles from approaching any closer than forty feet. Interest in the hieroglyphic panel and the map rocks had intensified and a sign on the road near lower Chalk Creek advertising the hieroglyphic panel was not helping preserve the site!

Leonard then set out to get to the bottom of why the hieroglyphs and map rocks existed in the first place, wanting to prove their authenticity or that they were nothing more than a hoax. In

1981, Leonard had first recorded the Fillmore hieroglyph and, like most academicians, was convinced the glyphs were old sheepherder graffiti or perhaps even the work of some ancient tribe of nomads passing through. At that time, he didn't know just how old and important they really were!

But with new determination Leonard set out on a mission that would ultimately lead him to learn new and exciting things about the past and about the ancient inhabitants of North America!

Fighting mainstream academia was only part of the problem with getting the site on the National Antiquities Site list; he had to battle his own contemporaries in the Forest Service including its upper echelon! Steve Manning of the "Utah Rock Art Society" as well as contributions by Deb Greathouse of the Delta, Utah City Library, and this author helped in the process of authenticating the Chalk Creek site at Fillmore, Utah.

After a two-year investigation into the authenticity of the Fillmore panel and accompanying map rocks, Robert Leonard penned the following summary of his findings.

The Findings of Archeologist Robert Leonard

"The hieroglyphics near Fillmore, Utah, above Chalk Creek, are an anomaly to most archeologists and rock art specialists. The panel doesn't resemble any of the rock art in Utah that experts assume is: (1) prehistoric, (2) Native American or (3) historic if documented or inscribed with a date. However, very few of the rock art panels in Utah can be absolutely dated or affiliated to a specific culture if they lack primary documentation.

"The Chalk Creek hieroglyphics, which present primary documentation, consist of 4 rows of west-facing symbols. There are 24 symbols in total. The top row consists of a single symbol, a Mayan-looking skull, facing forward. The other 3 rows have profiles of people, a 'Lady Liberty' figure facing forward, hands, boots, socks, a house, a rectangle, parallel lines, circles, triangles and a capital 'M'.

"My assertion is that the antiquity of the hieroglyphics is

known to be at least 69 years old and may exceed hundreds of years. Evidence will be presented using 4 lines of documentation.

(1) A 1982 oral history describing the 1939 discovery of the hieroglyphics.

(2) A 1941 photograph.

(3) The presence of lichen over patina on the panel in 1941.

(4) The widespread geographic distribution of similar to identical hieroglyphics.

"Documentation and recording of the Chalk Creek hieroglyphics began as a result of Clifford Purcell's discovery of the Fillmore Panel in 1939. After stumbling on the 'picture writing' as he called it in his interview with Fillmore forest ranger station employees, Purcell enlisted the help of vocational archeologist, Frank Beckwith, of Delta, Utah to examine the panel and to photo-document the writings.

"Beckwith (1876-1951), was the owner-publisher of the Millard County Chronicle and possessed incredible drive and energy [Figure 3.2]. He was a photographer fascinated with rock art and took hundreds of photographs of Utah's many hieroglyphic panels, many of which are now in the Beckwith Collection, sponsored by the J. Willard Marriott Library at the University of Utah. In 1941, accompanied by Clifford Purcell, Beckwith took the first known photographs of the Chalk Creek hieroglyphics along with photos of 'Signature Rock', which are now located in the Beckwith Collection.

"When I called the Delta City Library to see if they had any materials about Beckwith, the librarian, Deb Greathouse, said 'yes, quite a bit, and he was my grandfather.' It was Greathouse who first located the 1941 Chalk Creek photograph for me to examine.

The Tale of the Lichen Colonies

"When I first studied an enlarged 1941 photo of the Fillmore hieroglyphics at Chalk Creek, I was astonished to see lichen all over the panel just as Purcell had described. Lichen is a slow-growing colony of alga and fungus. There are thousands of species of lichen and each grows at their own predetermined rate of growth, which can be influenced by climate. I was hoping for funds to contract a lichenometric specialist when I got an e-mail from Boyd Shaffer, naturalist and professor of art and biology at the University of Alaska and author of 'The Flora of South Central Alaska: A Handbook for the Identification of Vascular Plants' (1994).

"According to Shaffer, a large part of the lichen on the 1941 hieroglyphic panel is identified as **aspicilia cinerea**. This lichen is ashy-gray in color and can be thousands of years old. Lichen grows according to the presence of moisture. It is dormant during drought and springs to life during wetter periods. Air pollution also affects the survival of lichen colonies.

"When I first recorded in the hieroglyphics in 1981, the hieroglyphics appeared as they do now: lichen-free, clean and very modern-looking. One possibility for the disappearance of the lichen is air pollution. However, the Intermountain Power Plant was not on-line in 1981 and I-15 is four to five miles west. I believe some well-intentioned person damaged the hieroglyphics by scrubbing the lichen off of the panel and cleaning out the incised glyphs with a screwdriver or similar instrument.

"If you compare Beckwith's 1941 [Figure 3.4] photo with 2008 photographs of the hieroglyphics, the profile of the head with hair (fourth row, third from left) has a rear feature chalked by Beckwith when he photo-documented the panel with Purcell. Whoever cleaned up the panel did not scrape this feature. The 2008 photo clearly shows grooves with patina. This would suggest that the lichen grew over a layer of patina. If you look closely at the 1941 panel, you will see that Beckwith had a hard time chalking the outline of the symbols. Several symbols were missed altogether. I believe he had difficulty, even with Purcell present, because the glyphs were lichen-covered and faint. The presence and extent of the lichen may have helped Beckwith with his determination that the panel was around 500 to 600 years old.

The Signature Rock associated with the Fillmore Panel no longer shows the red, hematite handprint [in Figure 3.4]. In the mid-1960's this rock was loosened by a bulldozer when Jose Davila and his partner were working around the rock and fell shortly thereafter. It eventually found its way to a rock shop in Fillmore.

E. Geographical Distribution

"The Chalk Creek hieroglyphics are not unique in their appearance. According to Steve Manning of the Utah Rock Art Society (2008: personal communication), sites with similar to identical glyphs are found at Ogden, Nephi, Manti and Cedar City. Castleton (1979: 65, 91 and 115) has recorded the panels at Nephi, Fillmore and Cedar City.

"Manning has gone a step further in his investigations and has found similar sites in Colorado, Idaho, Utah, Nevada and California. He presents a 1958 University of California Paper (No. 65) as irrefutable evidence for the regional distribution of the style and many of the elements of the Chalk Creek hieroglyphics. In an impending publication, Manning will suggest that most, if not all, of the hieroglyphics throughout the West are associated with the 1840's–1850's expeditions of a famous explorer According to Manning, the symbols are nonsensical and mischievous.

National Register Eligibility

"Even though in appearance the Chalk Creek hieroglyphics are not unique, they have historical significance in terms of their possible antiquity and are evaluated as National Register-eligible under Criteria A, C and D.

"A: If this panel is hundreds of years old, the obvious question is who drew the hieroglyphics on it and why? If not the product of a Native American (American Indian), then other people who inhabited the West during this period must be suspect. Such people would include slavers, explorers, fur trappers, miners, and colonists made up of Americans, French, Chinese, Russians, Mexicans and

Spaniards. The fact that the hieroglyphics are not geographically unique suggests that a group or groups of people, from Colorado to California, may have been involved in creating something unexplainable from Colorado to California (S. Manning 2008: personal communication). This is a broad pattern of hieroglyphics is broad whose effects on Western history are presently unknown.

"C: The hieroglyphics represent the work of an early (?) artisan. Around 12 hieroglyphic sites have been found from Colorado to the Pacific coast. However, Chalk Creek is the first site that has temporal data pushing the creation of this panel back to at least 1941. In addition, at that time the panel was heavily encrusted with lichen covering the patina, which indicates an even deeper antiquity.

"D: It is obvious that this panel, by itself or in conjunction with the other 12 sites throughout the West, begs for future investigation. It does not fit into any of our "archaeo-cultural" assumptions about what was going on in the West during the 18th or 19th centuries. It also bypasses all of the rock art forms, designs and motifs we assume to be Native American. In a way, the Fillmore hieroglyphic site is not unlike the Norse settlement at L'Anse aux Meadows in Newfoundland, which has befuddled generations of Americans brought up believe that Christopher Columbus discovered North America.

"There are just too many unknowns to dismiss this site as simply 'fraudulent'. And even if less than the "truth", whatever that means, +50 years old fraud is history which records not only the good but the bad and the ugly. I can state with certainty that the Chalk Creek hieroglyphics are at least 69 years old and using Lichenometry, are most likely older. By the documentation of the University of California's Archaeological Survey, we can state that the California-Nevada panels date to at least 1948. The ALA-51 and SOL-16 panels actually have more symbols that are identical to the Chalk Creek renders than a hieroglyphic site in Ogden, Utah. (All presented out of context; the reader is lost; will need more clarification) This substantiates a 50 plus-year antiquity of the Fillmore Panel and the presence of a regionally widespread style of rock art.

"As for interpretation of the Fillmore Panel, I have no idea what this panel or those across the West mean. Interpretation of the two anthropomorphic petroglyphs behind the visitor's center at the Fremont Indian State Park are still unknown. One of the petroglyphs has horns, the other does not. These two glyphs are located near a single petroglyph that looks as if the human form within it is wearing a space helmet. Were these petroglyphs left by extraterrestrials? Before I will dismiss this theory I want solid proof that they weren't.

"And let's not lose track of the motivation behind the nomination of the Chalk Creek hieroglyphics for the National Register. Interpretation must be treated as an undertaking with potentially adverse effects. The hieroglyphic panel and the nearby Map Rock have been vandalized three times in recent years."[1]

The Transliteration of the Fillmore Panel

At one point I was asked by the Fillmore Ranger District Office to participate in the transliteration of the Fillmore Panel, a feat I deemed myself unworthy of since my epigraphic knowledge is somewhat limited. However, I went ahead with the project and enlisted the aide of some talented individuals whose names cannot be given here due to their positions in a very prestigious university. Their loss of tenure if their names were known would be inevitable since they have side-stepped mainstream academia when it comes to ancient or early explorers from Europe, Asia, and Africa before Columbus.

My correspondence with these individuals about the transliteration of the Fillmore Panel about the *who*, the *why*, and the *when* in regards to this panel lasted for many months. It also included hundreds of emails between Robert Leonard and me. Research was conducted and reviewed over and over again to come to a viable conclusion. We knew right away that the inscriptions were not a vernacular script.

Using members of the epigraphic community throughout North America I was able to extrapolate a viable understanding of this panel and similar panels throughout the West. After our researchers examined the inscriptions on the Fillmore Panel, they all agreed that it was not a fake but very genuine! There are several elements that insure this. For example, the "tied boot" glyph is a city place name. It is often found in the northern Mesoamerican central highlands and dates to about AD 600–800 or a little later. There is also a "low sandal" or "partly broken sandal" that sometimes accompanies the tied boot. Also common with these two inscriptions are a sort of "lizard dog" for "Techatuta" in western Jalisco.

The "tie" idea means that an overarching authority, in this case the "King of He," has authorized the subordinated or contracted trader leaders to make an inscription. In this case, the group in our inscription is referring to the authorizing leadership of the Eastern Woodlands Hopewell capitol city, "He" ca. AD 330–450. This also insures the inscription's genuineness. There are several of these "tie" inscriptions at Turkey Hill, near Tulsa, Oklahoma. These inscriptions are sometimes written in the Peutinger Itinerary western centers Italic-Italianized patois,[2] AD 300–470, also present in the name, "Dierdre" at Veleia, Cantabrian coast of Spain, and dating about AD 320. The Bat Creek inscription royal or sub-royal male name is also "tied" to "He" with the "He" "tie" written vertically across the main name.[3]

One of our epigraphers pointed out that four of the letter sign glyphs on the right end of the upper two lines look like they were added after Spanish symbols were used regularly. This is also often true at Turkey Hill. In the upper line, the last three letters read *ojo* or *eye* and are rendered differently.

One way for folks to claim that the inscriptions cannot be genuine is to add something to them and then claim the artifact is a fake. Several rock shelter art and epigraphy has been annotated later, often by 19th to early 20th century visitors. About two-thirds of the very sophisticated inscriptions at the Coal Creek-Bluff-Gold Mine-Comb Wash Zones in Utah have been altered or added to after 1850.

The hands on the Fillmore Panel represent verbs and are genuine, as are four other symbols that are main letters from Mandaic and Syria, and date to AD 400 scripts. The heads on the panel are indicated and named normally, as in the David Deal Calendar Stone of AD 325, and in the Tucson Crosses named heads (Figure 3.8).

After studying the panel for some time, our epigraphic researchers were finally able to declare the site a Trade Route stop-over that was governed by someone appointed by the ruler of "Tied Boot." Not only does the panel include Mesoamerican inscriptions, but also Egyptian-style and Pale Ink Buddhist script. Some have even speculated that Buddhists came to the Northern Frontier in search of wild cattle (bison) and "red deer" (elk) along with horses to train to ride and pull two-wheeled carts. These Buddhists most likely mined for gold and silver and built northern roads for trade routes.

This idea of Pale Ink Buddhists having come north for trade purposes can be further idealized by two more inscriptions that appear on a lone rock that faces north. The inscription is what most understand to be the Yin Yang sign with an ochre-colored hand-print inscribed with an "eye" in the palm. The Yin Yang has been traced back to the Mongolians who used this sign to indicate the passing from death to life. The symbol represents two fishes and indicates a circle or cycle of fish eating the tail of another fish, hence "resurrection." This sign has been discovered throughout North and South America. Whether or not it translates the same in these different areas is unknown.

The ochre hand inscription is very complicated and important overall to this site. The Buddhists and Bodhisattvas are often depicted with stylized hand gestures called *Mudras*. The word Mudras is Sanskrit for "seal" or "sign" and each Mudras has a specific meaning, sometimes used as a symbolic gesture during rituals and meditation. The "ahhaya" Mudras is an open right hand, palm out, fingers pointing up. The ochre-colored hand is a sign of association with physical properties including fire and blood; magnetism on hands and presences of self and others. This is Buddhist iconography; open right hand, palm out fingers facing upward (Figure 3.9).

Other Sites with Noteworthy Inscriptions

There are dozens of sites throughout the Americas with similar hand and eye inscriptions, minus the ochre-colored open right hand, which appears at the Chalk Creek site. In Moundville, Alabama on the Black River in Hale County more than two-dozen truncated earth mounds were constructed by the Hopewell Culture that include these hand and eye inscriptions (Figure 3.9). The first extensive excavation at this site was directed by Clarence B. Moore and recorded in the *Journal of the Academy of Natural Sciences of Philadelphia,* in 1888 which published two volumes dealing primarily with Moundville. On a piece of pottery within the mounds was discovered an inscribed skull, hand, and eye on its side about 3.5 inches wide. More such hand and eye artifacts have been discovered in and around the prehistoric Hopewell Mounds in the midwestern United States.

Not to be outdone, Mexico sports its fair share of hand and eye motifs. The hand and eye examples found there are not restricted to the eye being superimposed on the palm of the hand. Ancient Aztec motifs, at times, show fangs in conjunction with the eyes located on hands, feet, elbows, and knees. The faces and particularly the eyes tend to be placed on the wrist and ankle, rather than directly on the palm of the hand or the sole of the foot. Some sources state the goddess of earth, Tlatechutli, had eyes and mouths at every joint.

The inscription in Figure 3.10 was interpreted by Jose Davila in 1965 to be that of the Mormon prophet Moroni. Exploring the meaning of the eye we find that in some cases it represents divine light or sight, conveying the idea of "seeing" or "knowing." What looks to be the capital letter "M" attached to a horizontal line that attaches itself to the upper part of the eye has been a subject of controversy for a number of years. There are several possible meanings for this inscription. One possibility is that it represents the Roman numeral 1000, or could symbolize *MANOA*, a Hebrew word for "place of rest."

Still other research suggests that this inscription represents a high mountain dwelling found in some writings by the before-mentioned Bodhisattvas. Whatever it may convey to us we know one thing: it is very old and was inscribed by someone who understood its meaning and wanted to convey that meaning to others, both past and present. With the letter "M" attached to the eye the inscription could be translated as "glowing city of light high in the mountains." It can be authenticated by the "house" symbol on the main panel that means "pyramid" or "stele" and can be found in Egyptian and Peruvian steles.

The most controversial inscription on the Fillmore Panel is the top hieroglyph that sits alone. Jose Davila translated this glyph by breaking it down into a dozen singular glyphs. His summary of the glyph is as follows: "To dig out of the earth—precious [garlanded] everlasting mineral records [documents] which are housed in a natural stone chamber." However, it is my opinion that the glyph is that of a skull and not unlike the several similar skulls discovered on other comparable panels, as well as on pottery, shells, and bronze weaponry throughout in North America, particularly in the Moundville, Alabama area (Figure 3.11).

Meanings of the skull vary with customs and cultures but mostly the skull represents "death" and "mortality." The Mayan skulls often represented the days on their calendars.

Most everyone has heard of the famed "crystal skulls" that are supposedly ancient in origin. At one point, crystal skulls were allegedly used by a group of Mayan priests to decode or translate ancient copper tablets as small as the palm of the hand with the help of a supposed "translator" named Cloudpiler. Using a crystal skull, which had a small slit cut into its mouth, the translator would insert a copper tablet, and then stare down through the top of the skull at the copper tablet and wait for the characters to change into his language so he could read it and speak it to a scribe. It was high in the mountains of Utah that Cloudpiler used a crystal skull to supposedly write the work now known as "The Mentinah Archives" with the help of Cesar Padilla de Ramarra and Tui Xiu of Guatemala, Menemi Shen of Taiwan, and Porfiro Munoz de Xiu of Ethiopia.

The fate of the crystal skull used by Cloudpiler and its fantastic properties is anyone's guess and may be a fabricated tale, but it still wakens the mind to the possibilities that such a skull would have if placed in the right hands.

The skull found in the hieroglyphs at Fillmore we are inclined to believe represents "death and mortality." It is fair to say that this site at Fillmore is just a small piece of the larger puzzle when it comes to identifying early cultures in our region. Ancient artifacts discovered throughout America add more pieces to the puzzle and indicate further that this continent was most likely peopled by educated, intelligent cultures that possessed the knowledge to manufacture certain types of items such as the one we discuss in the next chapter.

NOTES

1. Taken from an email from Robert Leonard. Printed with permission in its entirety.
2. Peuinger's Dictionary translation center in Holland, referring to Italian slang.
3. The famous Bat Creek Stone had been excavated by the Smithsonian Mound Exploration Program in 1885, and erroneously identified by Cyrus Thomas. In the 12th Annual Report of the Bureau of Ethology in 1894, as "Cherokee Writing," is now being exhibited in Delaware in a Cherokee,

or Indian collection even though it has been proven to be writing in Paleo-Hebrew.

CHAPTER IV
ANCIENT ARTIFACTS

ALONG THE OLD TRADE ROUTE FROM THE GULF OF MEXICO, AND where the Spanish once hauled gold and silver back to Santa Fe, age-old artifacts lay buried beneath the soil that was then pounded by hooves of donkeys, mules, horses, and cattle driven by the Spanish and various Indian tribes that later inhabited these same route locations. Little did most of them realize the history they trod over!

Along a lonely stretch of highway hundreds of years after the ancient traders had left western North America and after the Spanish quit coming north in search of mineral wealth, a crew boss for the Utah Department of Transportation was working alongside Highway 6 in Carbon County when he made a startling discovery buried a few feet deep in the highway's right of way!

The crew boss, Eugene Aagard, worked hard at his job laying oil and asphalt down lonely stretches of Utah highways in some of the bleakest areas imaginable! It was in the mid 1960s, while working on Highway 6 between Price and Green River that Aagard made this important discovery—an ancient stone oil lamp

(Figure 4.1, 4.2)! This discovery would forever change his way of thinking about who came to Utah first!

Battling Current Mindsets in Academia

Once Aagard made his fantastic discovery, he took the object home and put it on a shelf. He said the lamp was laying off the road in the bottom of the barrow pit.

It was many years later that a renewed curiosity in the lamp began. Aagard's grandson, Kevin Bess, took an interest in finding out more about his grandfather's mysterious old lamp. In April of 2006, Bess contacted Duncan Metcalfe, an associate professor of archaeology at the University of Utah, who Bess hoped might be able to shed some light on the lamp. Bess sent Professor Metcalfe an email giving as much detail and information as possible with some photographs of the lamp.

After a few days Professor Metcalfe responded. The following is his report:

Hi Kevin.

I've looked at the photographs and the short answer is I haven't seen anything like it. Which isn't saying a whole lot since there are a lot of objects I've never seen. Still . . . it looks vaguely Arctic in its design elements and shape. The hole through its base looks especially interesting since it appears to be cylindrical from the pictures. That type of hole is very, very difficult to make with a stone tool, but pretty easy with steel. That would place it in the historical period, but with respect to function and origin, I really don't have a clue.

I don't really know what to suggest. It is the common problem with questions like yours. It doesn't appear local, either in form, decoration or with respect to anything I've ever seen. So I'd guess it was brought in by someone and lost or tossed in the area where your grandfather found it. If it was found eroding from a cut bank or creek I'd probably suggest you bring it into the museum so I could look at it under a microscope. If it were found in an area with a lot of Fremont ceramics in buried deposits, then it would suggest it was local and I just haven't seen a similar example. Sorry, but context is everything when it comes to researching such things, especially fairly unique specimens.

Push comes to shove, I might try sending the digital photographs to one of the large coastal auction houses (Southerbys, Christys, etc.) and see if you can get their opinion. They are the folks who tend to staff the "Antiques Road show" and have much wider experience than I do. Sorry I couldn't be more help.

(signed) Best Duncan.

So Bess took it to *Antiques Roadshow* and he was told that it was a copy or a fraud of the real deal! As it turned out Kevin Bess more or less gave up on the lamp until his grandmother saw an article in the paper about me.

In May of 2008, Mary Aagard brought the lamp to my home. I examined it for hours before I came to the conclusion that it was in fact authentic. She told me that she had been told that it couldn't have been manufactured in Utah because it was made from alabaster. Whoever told her that had no knowledge of the vast alabaster deposits in Utah. We still don't know if it was made in Utah but we do know it was left in Utah.

Not far from where this lamp was found is the now famous "Range Creek Fremont Culture Encampment" that was once owned by Waldo Wilcox who sold his ranch in Range Creek to the Utah Division of Wildlife Resources. Wilcox decided that he was too old to care for the canyon properly so he sold it. Range Creek holds some of the most pure archeological evidence of the mysterious and enigmatic (so called) Fremont Indians in the Great Basin! We have to ask the question if these ancient people had commerce, or traded with other peoples who manufactured the lamp, or if it was perhaps something they themselves discovered and lost just a few miles west of their hidden homeland in Range Creek.

Most historians, archeologists, and educators teach that when an ancient artifact is discovered within the confines of North America it "had" to have been either a trade item or was brought from "the old country" and lost only to be rediscovered by illegal prospectors or treasure hunters.

This mindset is hard to change. Even with hard evidence, some people will not acknowledge the fact that North America has been home to countless cultures over thousands of years. These ancient people came and went leaving evidences of their existence, as we may presume with the Aagard oil lamp.

W.H. Holmes wrote a paper for the Bureau of American Ethnology around 1898 or 1899. Part of that report was edited by *Ancient American* Publisher Wayne May and published in his magazine (Volume 8 number 52). Holmes described aboriginal pottery discovered in the eastern United States. In his article he said,

> It is clear that this ware [meaning pottery/lamps] was not made by one but by many tribes, and even by several linguistic families, and we may fairly assume that the group is regional or environmental rather than tribal or national. It is a product of conditions and limitations prevailing for a long time throughout a vast area of country. As to the modern representatives of the pottery-making peoples, we may very reasonably look to any or all of the tribes found occupying the general region when the whites came—Algonquian, Siouan, Muskhogean, Natchesan, and Caddoan.

It is clear from Holmes's claims that with these many nations and their knowledge of pottery-making, they very well had the ways and means to produce all kinds of pots, vessels, lamps, and effigy models.

There have been published reports of ancient-style lamps being found in the Midwest of the United States. Thousands of objects dubbed as "frauds," "fakes," and a host of other titles, crowd storerooms in basements of museums and universities across North and South America. How does one explain how terra-cotta lamps used by ancient peoples wound up in America's heartland? What of the Ohio lamp, Wisconsin lamp, Roman lamp, and Utah lamps?

Were they brought here by travelers from the old countries, or were they manufactured here in America?

How do we explain the Michigan Tablets or Burrows Cave and Brewer's Cave, or the numerous rock writings and dolmens left here? How do we explain the marvelous oral histories of our American Indian friends that never change over hundreds of years? How can mainstream academia dismiss all of this and claim that the North and South American continents were peopled by immigrants who crossed a land bridge from Russia? It is truly mind-boggling!

Figure 4.4 is a photo of artifacts discovered near Manti, Utah. These artifacts alone give testimony of ancient cultures from at least 12,000 years ago.[1]

In issue number 90 of *Ancient American Magazine* the following article appeared which suggests the Brewer's Cave Story may very well be more truth than fiction! This article is reprinted here with permission so the reader can understand how carbon 14 dating helps date ancient artifacts.

> Radiocarbon Dating of Bark Sample From Brewer's Cave, Manti Area, By Steven E. Jones Professor of Physics, Brigham Young University, January 20, 2005:
>
> A number of stone boxes, covered with bark and pitch, were discovered by John Brewer in Manti, Utah, area nearly fifty years ago [see Figure 4.6]. While the authenticity of these discoveries has been the subject of intense controversy, radiocarbon dating of the bark has not previously been performed by archaeologists or other scientists. This oversight is striking, since an accurate radiocarbon age would do much to ascertain whether the artifacts are ancient, or modern manufacture (as claimed by some archaeologists).
>
> Here we report the results of the first radiocarbon dating of a bark sample from one of these stone boxes. The sample was provided originally by John Brewer. The bark was brought by J. Golden Barton to Professor Steve E. Jones of Brigham Young University on March 3, 2004, under the

auspices of the Ancient Historical Research Foundation. The sample was examined then taken to Prof. Stephen Nelson and David Tingey, both of the BYU Department of Geology, for dating using the BYU radiocarbon-dating system.

The bark sample was cleaned with acetone then propanol, then subjected to acid and base treatments. These steps were necessary to remove humic acids and residues from bacteria and other organisms, which could introduce fresh carbon 14 and thus produce a more recent (incorrect) age. After these standard procedures, essentially just cellulose from the bark remained. The cellulose material was subjected to standard chemical processes, finally to produce liquid C6H6 (benzene) which was placed into a vial with a scintillant. This carbon-barring vial was then placed into two separate scintillation counter instruments to record the carbon-14 radioactivity of the carbon sample

Both instruments gave essentially the same radiocarbon age for the Brewer Cave bark sample. The Guardian instrument provided an age of approximately 2161 years BP (Before Present). Since this age seemed incredibly old to the scientists doing the age analysis, the Brewer-bark sample was placed into Quantalus 1440 ultra-low background detector. This instrument includes 1500 pounds of lead to block cosmic ray interference. The sample was then analyzed ten times, at different times of the day to avoid the possibility of error. The final result confirmed the age determined by the Guardian instrument:

Precent modern carbon: (75.9 +/- 0.6) Radiocarbon age: (2161 +/- 70) BP Calibrated age (2 sigma): 5 BC to 390 BC. With a radiocarbon age of 5 BC to 390 BC, the Brewer-bark sample is thus scientifically demonstrated to be very old. The Brewer findings (if further verified) could force archaeologists to re-write currently accepted history of the area. It is extremely unlikely that the boxes in question could have been covered with bark this old by an alleged hoaxer, for that would require the individual to find intact bark that was already two thousand years old. Rather, the bark was evidently used anciently and preserved by pitch used to seal it

> and by its being kept in a rather dry-cave environment.
>
> The bark used to cover the stone box in question is indeed ancient. It is the opinion of this researcher that the findings and claims of John Brewer should be re-examined in light of this new, positive evidence for the antiquity of these boxes. It would be highly desirable to re-open the cave where the box was found, with certified archaeologists present (such as Jon Baxter of the Ancient Historical Research Foundation). Finding similar artifacts in their original undisturbed context would allow final verification of John Brewer's claims.

In a 2006 issue of *Ancient American Magazine,* Wayne May published a short report I sent him regarding a small, metallic-like lamp I discovered in a vein of carbon in northern Utah. How did it get there? In addition to Aagard's lamp, we now have discovered a lamp of a totally different design found in Utah (Figure 4.3). Again, it begs the question: How did it get there?

Oil lamps of stone and metal have been uncovered all through the Adena/Hopewell sphere area. This lamp is an example of marble construction. The handle and stopper are missing. The black covering is carbon from usage of the lamp.

Our colleagues in the archaeological community researched as to the origins of the ancient lamp I found, the one that Aagard discovered, and others spanning the North American continent, and have come up with countless theories. However, we believe one theory stands out above the rest: that oil lamps of this type belong to the Hopewell Culture. The Hopewell Culture was an elaboration and extension of the Adena mound-building culture (800 BC–AD 200). Hopewell art, burial ceremonies, and so forth, were more flamboyant than that of the earlier and more primitive Adena.

The Hopewell created some of the finest craftwork and artwork of the Americas! Most of their works had some religious significance, and their graves were filled with them. Beside the dead were placed beads, birch bark scrolls, ear and finger rings, metal figures, necklaces, ornate carvings made from wood or bone, painted mosaics, decorated ceremonial pottery, and pendants. Some graves were lined with woven mats, mica (a flaky, clear mineral), or stones.

To add more credence to our theory about the Hopewell culture being the creators of the curious oil lamps, I enlisted the help of a good friend, Robert W. Leonard, archeologist for the Fish Lake National Forest headquartered in Richfield, Utah. Leonard alluded to the idea that the oil lamp Aagard found may have come by way of the Mogollon Plains tribes but suggested I take the artifact to Lane Richens and Rich Talbot at the Office of Public Archeology at Brigham Young University in Provo, Utah. I had previously toyed with that idea but because Robert suggested it, I decided to go ahead.

On June 11, 2009 I made an appearance at the office of Richens and Talbot at BYU and had a meeting with Talbot and Richens. They examined the lamp and exclaimed that neither had ever seen anything quite like it. My suggestion that it could be Hopewell raised an eyebrow but nothing else. I proposed that the object might have been manufactured in Utah since alabaster is quite common here. Lane Richens rebutted that remark by saying the artifact was not from Utah. "Perhaps it came from the Middle East," he remarked. I hoped for additional information from the two archaeologists, but little more was said concerning the lamp.

It must be concluded that lamp was a trade item and was accidentally lost along the old trade route. However, members of the Church of Jesus Christ of Latter-day Saints might believe that it was lost by either a Nephite or Lamanite en route from the East to the West, presumably on their way to Sanpete Valley, Utah. There are ample sites that suggest an ancient culture lived in the valley about the same time as the reign of the Nephite/Lamanite period (circa 600 BC-AD 400). Sanpete Valley is situated about two and a half hours south of Salt Lake City.

"The dogmatic arrogance of so many modern archaeologists is due for a severe shaking. For they, like some of our learned professors at esteemed universities, are apt to forget that the bounds of knowledge are often advanced not by professionals or savants in learned societies and associations, but by the less assertive and generally undistinguished amateurs, laymen, and modest investigators."[2] This holds true, as well, in the discovery of dolmen stones of which we discuss next.

Notes

1. Shaffer, *Treasures of the Ancients*, 1–56.
2. Courtesy of Wayne May, publisher and editor of *Ancient American Magazine*.

CHAPTER V
DOLMENS

THE TERM "DOLMEN" COMES FROM THE OLD BRETON WORD meaning "stone table" or "table rock." Best known for their strange, if not bizarre appearance, they are chief in megalithic[1] monuments and are considered to be paramount in the megalithic family.

In England, Ireland, and France ancient dolmens of various sizes can still be seen today. A dolmen is usually meant to be a memorial to a chief or to some person or event of great importance and takes the form of a huge boulder, sometimes weighing tens of tons or more. This large boulder is supported by three to six smaller stones, leaving a void beneath the larger stone. Some of these smaller stones are conical in appearance and lift the larger stone off the ground from about six inches to as much as to two feet.

Dolmens discovered in the Americas were startlingly similar to those of European design. The oldest known examples of dolmens date back to around 4500 BC. Some scientists have tried to claim the dolmens are nothing more than glacier debris. However, that doesn't explain their strange formations and locations! While some rock mounds do in fact look as if they have been piled on top of each other in a fashion near those of constructed dolmens, they are, instead, the product of ice movements called "erratic."

Dolmens were first discovered in the New World in places like New Hampshire, New York, Massachusetts, Maine, and parts of Nova Scotia. These dolmens have been linked to the Vikings, who emigrated from northern Europe to Vineland (northeastern area of North America). However, the dolmens don't only show up on the East Coast of North America!

High on a ridge-line near Fish Lake on Fish Lake High Top Plateau twenty miles southeast of Richfield, Utah are two ancient dolmens. Discovered by Randy and Wanda Lewis, these dolmens are a standing witness to ancient inhabitants who used them for worship or as memorial monuments.

In 2007, Forest Service archeologist Robert Leonard and I made the trip to Fish Lake with the Lewises to investigate the dolmens and to authenticate the find. It is without question a marvel and a feat for the ancient dolmen creators to have set these giant boulders on the ridge (Figure 5.1). Lichen growth on the rock suggests that they have been in this position for over 1000 years!

Approximately two miles south of the dolmens are several rock monuments similar to those discovered by the Lewises. Alignment of certain monuments with the dolmens suggests the area was once used for ceremonies during solstice periods. Thinking this was just an oddity and not widespread in this area, we decided it must have been either a copycat culture or even a full-blown conspiracy to create confusion in the academic community.

No more than a month later, three gentlemen from Sanpete County, Utah contacted me about a fantastic discovery in their county. (These three gentlemen asked to remain anonymous for this publication.) A meeting was arranged where we could sit down to look at photographs they had taken of an area off the beaten path in a remote part of the county. The photos revealed dolmens of various sizes and shapes (Figure 5.2)[13]! It was truly a magnificent find! It was decided by these three men that they would take me on a trip to the site as long as I would promise to keep silent about the site.

On a hot summer day in July 2008 they took me to see the dolmens. To witness such an old and strange-looking dolmen in this remote region of the county was very exciting and educational. Large Juniper trees had grown through some of the monuments and lichen covered every inch of some of them. It was obvious these dolmens were ancient and had not been disturbed since the inhabitants of this area left many centuries ago. Strange as it was, one dolmen had a Patriarchal Cross symbol carved deep into it. Investigation continues in this area and it is without question one of the mysteries of ancient America!

The Significance of Dolmens in America

The reader may ask here what makes these dolmens so important to our history. They are important because they simply don't belong! Or do they? Now, is it not extraordinary that in America—in particular New England and other eastern locations—we can recognize all the main types of megalithic structures that our European colleagues report from Europe (Figure 5.3)? Our structures are associated in most cases with pagan Celtic origin but still, what are these strange dolmens and megalithic structures doing in Utah? Those questions prey on the minds of the historically curious continually! To add to this mystery, dozens of megalithic monuments have been discovered south of Fish Lake in Utah's high plateau country east of Richfield, Utah (Figure 5.4).

In the 1950s a man by the name of Lorenzo Larsen herded sheep in the Loa area of southeastern Utah from Fish Lake Mountain to the high country of the Aquarius Plateau on Boulder Mountain. Larsen, like most sheepherders spent the whole of his day tending sheep, shooting predators, talking to his horse and dogs, and generally living in the wilds nature has to offer. He alleged during his more boring days that he decided to construct animals and "suggestive" human forms from the local lava rock that covers most of that high country. Larsen claimed to have created over one hundred of these rock megalithic structures. One Bureau of Land Management employee toppled several of the more suggestive human-looking shapes.

In 2009 an investigation was undertaken by several individuals to gather information on the claims made by Larsen. After visiting several of the larger rock formations it was very evident that one man or even two men could not have lifted the very heavy and awkward lintel stones that grace most of these types of structures. The location of these formations presented another problem with Larsen's claim. Creating such structures, even today, would require machinery to get into and stack such heavy rocks to their position. With Larsen's claims debunked, we are now presented with a new mystery about how these megalithic structures came to be in this part of the United States, who the real creators were, and how they managed to accomplish this amazing feat!

While it is true that dolmens and numerous ancient structures dot several areas within Utah, creating exciting myths and mysteries, many of our sister states, as well, have their own stories to tell relating to such structures. These myths and mysteries, found all across the United States are many and widely spread, as we will see in our next chapter.

Notes

1. *Megaliths* are huge rock edifices or monuments constructed for a number of reasons.

CHAPTER VI
BURROWS CAVE

To further support the fact that the Americas were inhabited by ancient races, we have the story of a fantastic discovery by Illinois State Militia Colonel Russell Burrows during an excursion in the hills of southern Illinois in 1982.

Burrows lived in Olney, Illinois and belonged to the Illinois State Militia. The militia had been set up as an organization dedicated to the preservation of history. All his life, Burrows had been thrilled by caving, or spelunking as it is called by professionals. He could not have known that a cave he would literally fall into would have such a great impact on his life.

According to Burrows he liked to explore places that had been untouched for many years. He always listened to rumors and stories about homesteads, robberies, bandits, and even treasure hunts for lost Spanish gold! However one story got his attention in particular, so he began searching an area in Marion County, Illinois near Skillet Creek.

Burrows wasn't too concerned that the property he was about to enter was privately owned. He entered the woody acreage to begin his hunt for an old homestead, but day after day he would come away empty handed.

Over the course of a few weeks, Burrows became familiar with the area and said it had very distinct features that were easy to remember. He said he liked this area because it afforded him a nice place to sit down and eat his lunch, it being an edge of a bluff. After eating his lunch he would just step down onto a flat stone and be on his way again.

It was in April of 1982 when Burrows found that the flat rock he had stepped on so many times wasn't just a "step"! As he stepped down onto the stone on that day in April, instead of stepping on the center of the rock like he had done so many times before, he stepped on the edge of the flat rock and caused it to flip over, dropping Burrows down through a hole to a large room below!

Burrows was frightened out of his wits but managed to hang onto the edge of the hole somehow! The hole was about thirty inches across at the top and less than six feet wide at the bottom. Letting himself slide down, he hit the floor of the pit.

Once at the bottom he was startled to discover a very large face carved into the wall of the pit! Looking around in the dim light Burrows saw many other figures cut into the walls. Strange forms and symbols adorned the other walls in the cave.

Burrows knew he had stumbled onto one of, if not *the* greatest archeological and historical discovery in North America! The old homestead he had been looking for was now a distant memory—for now he had at his disposal a find that couldn't be matched!

Burrows crawled his way out of his temporary would-be tomb and headed for home. He was both excited and scared—who would he trust to tell his story to? What would he do next? He decided to go back to investigate the site. This he did over and over, making one exciting discovery after another!

Burrows mapped out the cave, its entrances, side passages, crypts, and areas of artifacts. He discovered that the cave was not only a tomb but a cache of weapons, gold coins, amulets, tools, death masks, ceremonial instruments, and many other phenomenal items (Figures 6.1–6.8).

Burrows was concerned that his find would be declared a fraud and felt he must confide in a friend whom he could trust, an anthropologist at Eastern Illinois University, located in Charleston, Illinois named Leon Brown.

Burrows made an appointment to see Professor Brown and appeared at his office with some of the artifacts he had removed from the cave. Of course the first thing Brown asked Burrows was "Where is the cave?" Of course Burrows refused to tell the cave's location.

Pressuring Burrows for more information, Brown pushed Burrows to the point where he almost got up and left, but because he wanted answers he stayed his ground. After the professor had taken a close look at the artifacts, he told Burrows he doubted they were very old but he would look into the matter further and let him know.

Burrows had hardly made it home when the phone rang. It was Professor Brown telling him that he had news about his artifacts! Burrows was excited and anxious to hear the news. However, what he learned wasn't exactly good news. Brown had called the State Archaeologist at Champaign, Illinois and described the artifacts to her. The woman's response was "Oh, I know what those are. They were made by a cult in southern Illinois about a hundred years ago and they must have hid them in caves or buried them."

Burrows was dumbfounded! How on earth could she make that determination by a simple phone call? Brown stuck by her saying, "She is a very sharp person and has studied the history of Southern Illinois at length; she really knows what she's talking about."

This statement left a sour taste in Burrows' mouth! He was determined to find out what he had in his possession and now he had to think of something to prove that what he had found was not a cache of toys placed there by a cult!

For a while Burrows would sneak into the cave and rummage along the floor, side tunnels, and hidden passageways finding all sorts of stone tablets and amulets. He brought several thousand of them out and horded them away at his residence.

He knew a woman by the name of Thelma McClain who ran a small antique and curio shop in Burrows' hometown of Olney. McClain had all sorts of arrowheads, stone axes, and other such Indian artifacts for sale. Burrows decided to see if he could sell some of his stones to her, so one day be brought in about twenty stone tablets and amulets for McClain to see. Gleefully she agreed to put them on display. She asked Burrows where he had gotten them so that when people came in she could at least give some sort of historical background on them. All Burrows would tell her is that they came from a cave in Illinois.

A man, who would later become one of Burrows' greatest allies, John A. Ward (or Jack as he was called by friends), came into the picture about this time. Ward, an author and historian and curator of the Sonofobac Museum in Vincennes Illinois, saw the Russell Burrows stones at the little store and got very excited! Ward had written about ancient scripts and had even helped decipher some found on rocks in the Midwest.

Ward was anxious to get together with Burrows so a meeting was arranged. Burrows was introduced to Ward and discovered that he could decipher ancient script. Burrows felt as if a door had opened for him, clearing the way to finally get some answers.

With the excitement of finally being able to realize what he might have, Burrows was however, soon dealt a blow by a man named Barry Fell, a professor of ancient history who had dedicated his life to reading and deciphering ancient scripts. Fell was an epigrapher, explorer, and scholar of ancient scripts. He was also the founder of the Epigraphic Society. When Fell heard about the Burrows Cave artifacts he wanted photos as soon as possible or hands-on examinations of the relics.

Fell received drawings of some of the artifacts and immediately claimed that the drawings were copies from objects included in his book *America B.C.* Fell took great pride in his work and it bothered him to think someone was taking credit for what he had been doing for so long.

Soon Fell was able to view actual photographs of some of the stones taken from Burrows Cave and decided to print an article about them in the 1990 *Epigraphic Society Occasional Papers*, (vol. 19):

> On October 22, 1986 Ms. Virginia Hourigan kindly forwarded to me a series of photographs of engraved tablets of some unstated material said to have been found in a cave in Illinois known as Burrow's [Burrows'] Cave, whose location is secret. Ms. Hourigan authorized me to report on the translations of the inscriptions. In my reply to her, however, dated Oct. 29, 1986, I expressed my regret at having to inform her that the tablets are "meaningless fakes of very modern origin, in which childish drawings and absurdities were applied to surfaces that obviously had required an advanced technology to produce."
>
> In a subsequent letter Ms. Hourigan forbade me to use the photos, of which she claimed the copyright, so I could not report to the Epigraphic Society on the matter. Since then I have received from James Whittall, Harvard graduate and archaeologist to the Early Sites Research Society, drawings that he was permitted to make by Mr. Russell Burrows, dealing with the same plates, and as these are not subject to copyright, I am notable to report upon them.
>
> I have to state that the plates illustrated in this report are meaningless combinations of pseudo-ogam and Phoenician and Libyan letters, apparently copied from various papers I have published in ESOP or in my books, but so jumbled and utterly unlike the originals as to imply modern incorporation of my results by other persons. I draw attention in particular to Figure 3 on the following page, in which an erroneous version is given of the elephant plate originally excavated at the airport in Cuenca, Ecuador. The original report of this plate is shown in Figure 1, (by Charles Berlitz), and an erroneous version in Figure 3 included in my book "America B.C." (1976). Soon after I discovered the error and corrected it as shown in Figure 4, in the NEARA Journal for 1976 figure. Figure 2 shows a sketch by Gloria Farley of a stone or

> tablet recovered from Burrows Cave, recorded the erroneous version of my 1976 figure. Thus I date this Burrows Cave figure to 1976 or later, showing it to have no antiquity but merely an irrelevant and improbable Illinois version of an inscription properly to be related to Ecuador.

According to Fell, Burrows was nothing short of a shyster and would stop at nothing to gain a reputation of being a great explorer. In Fell's eyes, Burrows was an exploiter of artifacts whether authentic or not.

Undaunted, Burrows gave John Ward the stones to study and after some serious examination he told Burrows that the strange writing was in fact ancient Egyptian-Libyan script and it was most likely left there by a people who migrated from those two countries in the seventh century BC. Ward told Burrows that he thought he could decipher the script and that he had already written a book on the subject of ancient cultures in the Wabash Valley, (Indiana and Illinois) and had experience in this field.

Burrows decided to trust John Ward and visited with him again some months later. The idea of obtaining some of the cave's stones for a museum was proposed and Ward offered Burrows a sizeable sum for his collection. Burrows had exhausted his funds going to and from the cave so extra money for his adventures was welcomed.

For a time Burrows brought out more stones and artifacts for the museum and soon the collection was very sizable. After a time, Ward and his partner, Norman Cullan, asked Burrows to just bring in his stones on loan only since they had acquired so many already.

Ward pressed Burrows for the location of the cave but Burrows would not reveal it to him or anyone else for that matter, but did say that he took his brother-in-law to it once and that it was "a big mistake!"

Ward was intent on meeting the landowner of the property where the cave was located. Burrows had to do something about that so he, according to some sources, created a fictitious landowner, by the name of George Neff, who seemed never to be available for one reason or another.

Letters To and From the Mysterious Mr. Neff

In an attempt to bring Neff to the front, Ward continued to ask to meet the landowner and Burrows produced a bogus letter supposedly written by Neff in an attempt to pacify Ward:

Feb. 1, 1985

Dear Russell:

I hope this finds you well and not to[o] cold. I am really happy here in the sunshine. Wish you were here, we could go fishing. Russell, the reason I am writing you and not calling on the telephone is so you can't use your winning ways on me, I'm joking.

Seriously, I have become aware of the new problems you are having with that bunch in Vincennes. I don't know for sure what it is they want for their museum but if this letter don't do for them then they can go to hell because I won't give anything else or meet anyone. But by this letter I am giving you the right to all the things you have found so far on my place. They are yours to do with as you want as I have no interest in such things.

Russell I hate doing this because you have become a true friend to me and Daddy. But the folks down there are really upset because I agreed to sell you the holler. I really fear for you with those people because some of them would just as soon shoot as talk and I'm sure you know why. Because if that and the other troubles you are having and because sooner or later you are going to need to take some collage [college] folks in there to see the place I am going to have to withdraw my offer to sell to you. I will allow you time to get all your stuff out and for sure any more fancy rocks you have found up to now. But after the first of March it must be closed up and I won't allow anyone at all to go in there.

You can use this letter as your authority to own what you have found. Please don't show the envelope so people will know who I am and where. Also I am signing with my first name, Initial and last initial to keep who I am a secret.

Your friend,

George W. N.

P.S. I expect you to respect my wishes. Some day I'll make it up to you.[1]

According to some sources Burrows had to keep up the façade to protect the cave. In addition, Burrows penned a note describing a meeting he had with Neff a year later. Burrows had drawn a map to the cave and kept going to the cave over the course of the year 1985. In the note, he finally persuaded the fictitious George Neff to agree to sell off some more of the artifacts.

Mr. Neff called me on the morning of Thursday, January 2, 1986 and requested that I meet with him at O'Fallion. At this meeting I found him to be very angry. The reason being that all but one of the promises made to him had been broken. He knew that Mr. Ward has in his possession a map pinpointing the exact location of the caves as well as his property. He knew also that his name is known as well as the entrust deed with certain banks. He also knows that my recovery work has not been supported as was promised and that I had gone from $1,800.00 to just under $4,000.00 in the red. I DID NOT REVEAL THESE THINGS TO HIM![2]

In a note to Burrows, the mysterious Mr. George Neff said the following:

I am really mad about this. I don't know why those people can't keep their word and live up to what they agree to. Ward didn't tell me about, I won't meet him till spring. But I have someone watching for me that you guys will never believe and they keep me informed. What you should have done when he kept laying out those maps was to just say NO, I gave my word! I think you got suckered into it because you are to easy and trusting. I don't like this business of you going in the hole as old as your are, if he's not buying those rocks now, well it is just going to get worse. How are you going to pay back the loans you have made to keep their work going. Those guys in Vincennes must really think I am dumb not to see where they are going with this. I intend giving this place to them the first week of April providing this gets sorted out now. I want you to type this up and take it over to Ward, after he reads it I want him to initial it so I know that you didn't try to keep from hurting his feelings. I am giving you back the piece of marble you gave me and I want you to offer it for sale to him, then I want you to tell me what he gave you for it. If I have to bale you out of this I will but if that happens then I'll know for sure there is a rooster trying to lay eggs. If those guys are broke then the queen of England is a hooker. I am privy to that information and I can tell you that Ward has a real good savings and Cullen has been a lot more helpful than we can expect. You just do what I'm telling you to, when you get back from over their, call my neph[p]ew and I'll get word from him, then we will meet. Now, do you need any money now? No, O.K. I don't believe you but O.K. I can see where you are coming from there.[3]

This is a report of our meeting word for word concerning the cave project. We talked of other things but they are not related.

A few days later John Ward wrote the following letter to George Neff:

January 8, 1986

Dear Landowner:

Attached is a memorandum given to me by Russell Burrows, wherein I have signed it attesting that I have read it and it is to be delivered to you in order for you to know that I have read it.

Being a rural landowner myself, I can appreciate your viewpoint on being adamant that your property should remain the utmost secrecy as any disclosure of the cave's location could attract swarms of treasure hunters and undesirable people to encroach on your privacy. The why of our position is clearly your own desires, which I respect with the utmost adherence.

I wish to outline some of the problems I have encountered in upholding your viewpoint and insistence.

Everyone wants to rely on the opinion of such institutions as the Smithsonian Institution in Washington D. C. to validate their authenticity. Mrs. McLain, who bought a substantial number of the white marble slabs, sent Polaroid photos of some of the pieces and obtained a reply on August 10, 1983 that they were not of prehistoric manufacture. I have sent a set of better photographs to Dr. Barry Fell a professor emeritus of Harvard University, who now lives in San Diego, CA. I invited him to come at my express anticipation that on such as occasion you would permit Mr. Burrows to take him into the cave to verify its existence. Dr. Fell replied to me by letter that he would not undertake to examine the cave and its contents until someone else had verified that it is there and the secrecy is abated. He cautioned me that these artifacts MAY be forgeries or of recent manufacture and planted in the cave.

I sent a set of photographs to Mrs. Gloria Farley of Heavener, OK, who has found similar artifacts in a cave in Oklahoma, she consulted with Phil Leonard of the Western Epigraphic Society in Colorado, and he called me at his own expense and talked to me for an hour, and it was his opinion that they were not genuine or of ancient manufacture.

I went to the University of Kentucky to show some of them to Dr. Wm Y. Adams who spent two decades in Nubia on the Aswan Dam recovery project. He refused to make any documented opinion on them, but did not declare them to be fakes, but merely stated he had seen nothing like them along the Nile where he had worked.

I showed them to a Mr. Carlos Coliftis at Livingston, Ky. who had some very similar artifacts that had been found in a cave in Eastern Kentucky near the Virginia state line. He said a lot of the black artifacts like I showed him, were in the Kentucky Cave. Mr. Coliftis would not tell me where his cave was and would not disclose the name of the landowner, except that he lived in Indiana.

I took two pieces to Dr. John Patton, the Indiana State Geologist at Indiana University. He immediately assured me that it was what is called Numulitic limestone and that none was like it in North America. I left samples with him to analyze, and the laboratory report indicated that it was carbonate rock rather than Diorite and the white stone was marble which could have been obtained either in the United States or at various other places in the world.

My opinion is that the black hard stone is diorite and came from an ancient quarry in Nubia. I contend that the white marble is from a quarry north of Memphis at a place called Turah (Egypt.) The quarry there is of Mocottam Numulitic limestone hard enough to be classified as marble.

I had a close friend, Colonel Ray Hankins AF Reserved take a trip to Egypt and at Aswan, in a curios shop he found a pyramid paper-weight made of the same material. He asked the merchant what kind of stone it was and he said it was diorite and came from 600 miles further up the Nile in Nubia. I compared it with the stone from the cave and it's identical.

In spite of all the negative opinions of others, and in the absence of being able to authenticate it I have conducted my own research and am convinced that the artifacts are ancient manufacture. But who am I? I am not what any museum or institution would call an authority. I have just spent 50 years in the limestone business as a salesman, but I have studied rocks all over Southern Illinois and Southern Indiana having caused investors to open quarries at Mitchell, Indiana and Ullin, Ill. I was with the East St. Louis Stone Company 5 years, and with my Father in the material business for ten years, with the Mitchell Crushed Stone Co. for 30 years, I've marketed crushed stone from Anna, Illinois and Hopkinsville, Ky. I contend I know as much about limestone as anyone in the Midwest. The limestone on your place is of the McLeansboro group and strata of the Omega limestone the same formation at Omega where Gail McCarty of Egyptian Concrete Co. operated a quarry some 30 years ago. It is also the same formation from which a quarry operates at Dix. Now I contend that none of the local sources of limestone compares with the limestone slabs from the cave.

Over the last 18 months I have purchased from Mr. Burrows over $5,100.00 of the recovered artifacts, my associate and patron of the museum has purchased over $2,000.00 to be donated to Sonotabac Museum, others who purchased about $1,500.00 for their own *collections. These purchases were to help Mr. Burrows bear the expenses of exploration and to acquire sufficient array to study the inscriptions to establish a hypotheses of what those artifacts represent.*

The artifacts that I have purchased are my personal property and do not belong to the Sonotabac Museum or the Old Northwest Corporation. In addition to the artifacts from the cave, I have over $6,000.00 of my Indian artifacts on loan to the museum.

I have four adversaries on the Board of Directors of Old Northwest Corporation, who because Mr. Burrows refuses to divulge the cave's location or the name of the land owner, or no one has seen the cave or the contents in site, they are doubtful of the existence of the cave. I have been instructed by the four members of the Board to get the authentication of the artifacts or not show them at the Museum. The concept of peoples from Egypt colonizing the Ohio Valley and especially Vincennes is hard for them to swallow. Even the inscribed stones found on Knox County farm fields, which I have deciphered long before the cave became an issue, they take issue with, and simply do not believe. We must remember we have all been taught that Christopher Columbus discovered America in 1492, and the idea that colonist came here in 740 BC is too far out to be acceptable.

The school teachers teach the children that Columbus discovered America and then bring busloads of little minds to Sonotaback Museum and here a man named Ward, who is not an academia or of college degree, shows them that their school books are all wrong because some scratches on stones which look like plow marks are interpreted to be an ancient language called Ancient Libyan and they get it all confused with present day Libya and a Colonel Kadafy.

Among the stones that I have purchased from Mr. Burrows are sealing blocks from mastabas of Fourth and Fifth Dynasty aristocrats (2,600 B.C.) and it is my belief that they were taken out of tombs in the eighth century B.C., sold to Phoenician mariners for ballast, they then in turn traded them to the Mound Builder colonists for copper nodules which was mined from the glacier moraines near Attica, In.

The black artifacts are ceremonial pieces brought over by Nubian Traders in 726 B.C. Some are very crude spear points though some are highly polished. None of the spear points are marketable through the Indian Relic Traders, because they do not conform to accepted traditional shapes and of material attributed to locally established sources of flint or chert type of material. Other items of this material (diorite) are plate-like slabs usually oval in shape on which faces of warriors or chieftains are engraved. Some are also embellished with ancient script, some of which I have been able to translate, and many are in the stage of decipherment. There are also novelties in various shapes of animals, ships, knives, and many which are no doubt ceremonial artifacts but for what and to what meaning do they have?

Since 1947 I have maintained my own private office at 819 N. 4th Street, a duplex apartment one side I rent out, and the other is my office and storage space for my artifacts. It is not open to the public and the door is kept locked and I admit anyone on business only. The only people who have been in this office in over 3 years are my daughter and son-in-law who live in my house next door. I do not discuss anything about these artifacts with them, only family matters. The only other people to visit my office are Russell Burrows, Norman Cullen, the patron who has been also buying artifacts from Russell, a lady from Southern Knox County who came to buy some arrowheads, and her husband who sold me a 5" diorite ring he found in lower Knox Co. Mrs. McLain of Olney who came last week concerned with trying to learn of any developments of my authentication efforts, Russell came in as she was leaving. Outside of these people named there has been no one else here. Not even my wife.

In the memorandum handed me by Russell, to read and initial to be returned to you to be sure I read it. In the first paragraph (1) states that you know of a map pinpointing the exact location of your property. The only person to see the map was Russell Burrows.

I maintain a supply of aerial survey photographs of a lot of Illinois areas which I obtained in my resonance of various set up sites for contractors in highway work along the proposed work. This particular set is part of a set I assembled to study the proposed and cancelled out Helm Reservoir as proposed by the Wabash Valley Association. For ten years I was the Chairman of the Navigation Committee.

Early in my own research I wanted to try to theorize WHY these particular artifacts were in that cave. In October of 1984 I fancied that perhaps the Mound Builders wanted to return these wares to the Sun God. I began by setting on top of Sonotabac Mound at sunset and taking note of where the sun touched the horizon at sunset and charting this point of sunset on every evening from October 15 through November 15, charting every evening projecting it all across Illinois into Missouri on a big topo[graphical] map. Then I theorized that on November the 1st, their Holy Day of Samhain would probably be the alignment. I then retraced that same alignment back east, the line penetrated a bluff wall with inscriptions on it at Trinity Springs in Martin County, Indiana, the line continued through a town on the Ohio River called "Rising Sun", then on east into Ohio to the foot of the Great Serpent Mound at Peebles, Ohio. The western extension of that line went to Crystal Cave in Missouri. In other words the line of the Sun began at Peebles Great Serpent Mound passing over Rising Sun, passing by the inscribed cliff at Trinity Springs, passing over Sonotabac Mound to Crystal Cave. Since the slope of the land from just east of a point south of Iuka slope westerly to the Mississippi and from the same point south to Iuka the slope easterly is to the Wabash. This established for me the horizon, just east of where the November line of the sun might be the location of such a cave. The line of the sun on that date is just a ¼ mile north of your property. I then began looking on the standard plat map of your county and found no property owners name which bore the initials of GWN a signature on a letter you gave to Russell on February 1985. The most apparent tract was in trust to a bank. My concern to try and locate the cave's approximate location was to be a possible disaster route to get to Russell in case he got trapped and didn't show up home some evening. I also thought of the planning that would be necessary to get appropriate equipment in to remove the silt from the cave and just where we could have access for egress and engress if the cave were eventually given to the Old Northwest Corp.

Also in paragraph (1) there has been no promise of support to Russell Burrows to bear any fixed or open-ended amount to support his expenditures in the cave exploration. All that has been paid to him is agreed purchase prices for each item chosen to be purchased. I thoroughly understand that Mr. Burrows has his own internal expenses and is entitled to make profit for his labors and time, but there has been an assurance made to him for maintaining a level of profitability.

As I mentioned earlier, the object of my acquiring these artifacts was to assist Mr. Burrows in his expenses and time. My objective was to amass enough of the various artifacts to develop enough material to judge what they were, where they came from. My principal interests are those artifacts that bear inscriptions, in order that I may decipher their meaning to support a conclusion that would lead to someone of authority to authenticate them.

As to our living up to our word on what we agreed to do, I do not understand. The only contact in this entire matter has been through the utmost confidence in only one man, that being Russell Burrows. Other than him showing me a letter purporting to be from you, signed George W.N. you are utterly invisible. I have no assurance that you exist. I have no concrete evidence that there is such a cave. I have no idea what your reasons are to remain anonymous but that is your wish and I have respected it. I have been hoping to meet with you and talk eyeball to eyeball and discuss with you personally the manner of future developments suiting your wishes.

As to my being able to continue buying artifacts from Russell, please remember I am a retired person on Social Security and a very limited income. My role as Director of the Sonotabac Museum is that of a volunteer worker. I have no idea how I might be able to profit from my interest in proving that these artifacts are genuine ancient articles. I certainly do not have the financial ability to finance the full recovery from the cave. If you propose to give the contents of the cave to the Old Northwest Corporation, such an acquisition would require that I and we (ONC) would have to develop some means of funding to obtain a financial budget covering the expenses of such a project. This would have to be seeking grants from foundations, as the present financial position of the ONC is a very meek source of relying on membership dues and admission fees, which barely meet the cost of yearly operation. I was elected President of the Old Northwest Corp. with the thought in mind that I would be the one to go out and solicit grants. However, I have been so involved with the problem of trying to get the cave artifacts authenticated I have not been able to devote any time in funding solicitation.

Thirteen years ago the Old Northwest Corporation was involved in celebrating our part of the Nation's Bicentennial and it was through that effort that we acquired the property adjacent to the mound itself. I converted the modest dwelling on the property to a museum. Over the years I have filled four rooms with displays interpretative of civilization of the local mound builders and the museum became an interpretative center. Upon my seeing the artifacts from the cave, I became convinced that they were part of this mound builder group's ceremonial horde, and through interpretative displays prove that such people came from Egypt and Nubia. If the artifacts belong to any museum display, ours should be the one. I have filled every available space even on the floor, of artifacts I've purchased from Russell. I am limited by space and add very little more. I have stored some of them here in my personal office, and even here I am cramped for space.

I would now like to explain the concern of the four adversary Directors and explain their viewpoint regarding the artifacts that I've bought from Russell. They hold no animosity towards Russell Burrows other than they cannot understand the secrecy of who the landowner is and his determined refusal to reveal the cave location.

Three of the adversaries are teachers of history, one being a historical researcher and artist. A curator of the Lewis Library of Historical Collections at Vincennes University, who is also Chairman of the Board of ONC.., the third, is a history professor at Vincennes University. The three are more concerned with the French House, another museum property owned by ONC, than they are with the Sonotabac Mound & Museum. The fourth adversary is Vice President of Security Bank & Trust Co. who is treasurer of Old Northwest Corporation.

Now they all admit, that if we would authenticate these artifacts it would be the greatest thing that could happen to Old Northwest Corporation. They are not aware of your considering giving the cave's contents to Sonotabac Museum. If you could see fit to meet with them revealing your identity and assuring them that you have given Russell Burrows permission to remove these artifacts from the cave, the whole matter would clear up.

Their position is that suppose we go out and solicit funding for an expansion of the museum, based on the need for more space to display such a great archaeological find, build the addition with such solicited funding, display the artifacts and get a wonderful reputation for such exhibits, then down the road two or three years from now, someone shows up on the scene and claims to be the landowner or his heir and challenges our right to have them and sues the ONC for harboring stolen property and if such an occurrence caused the artifacts to be removed from the expanded museum and in that result the funding source for the museum expansion could come back on the Old Northwest Corporation for return of the funding granted.

I think you can see their concern especially when there is no documentary evidence to the contrary . . . I think you will agree that under the circumstances I have displayed complete confidence in Russell Burrows and I respect your wishes to remain anonymous.

Other than the Board's position as explained above as of the late fall of 1984 and one other time in the summer of 1985 when they insisted that I get the artifacts authenticated or remove them from the museum, there has been no discussion whatsoever at any board meeting. At that time I advised them that I was trying to get authentication, but it would take time. We only meet once a month. I do not plan to expose your intention to give the cave contents to the Sonotabac Museum until you authorize me to do so.

I am attaching a separate sheet of the list of Officers & Directors of Old Northwest Corporation for your information.

I am Very Truly Yours
(signed) John A Ward.[4]

The story of Russell Burrows and his alleged discovery would take volumes if all the letters and documents were brought to light. But it would be with great displeasure to read them all, since both the mysterious George Neff and Russell Burrows pen letters alike, and often use profanity and vulgar innuendoes.

Burrows Cave would be one of the greatest discoveries of all time *if* only greed hadn't played such a big part in it. Removal of artifacts from their resting place does more damage to authentication than anything else. The questions remain and the doubters are many.

The cave has been sealed shut and the ghosts are silent. Burrows only revealed the cave to one other trusted soul. Again, we have little to go on but stories! Over time this story will become a legend and will be embellished beyond belief! Will a cave of such significances ever be found again? Only time will tell.

Likewise with early discoveries in the same region of North America, shrouds of doubt and skullduggery played a key roll in the discoveries made that are now part of the Michigan Tablets that we will discuss in the next chapter.

Notes

1. Unsolicited information from a source not wishing to be identified. Original text.
2. Unsolicited information from a source not wishing to be identified. Original text.
3. Unsolicited information from a source not wishing to be identified. Original text.
4. Unsolicited information from a source not wishing to be identified. Original text.

CHAPTER VII
THE MICHIGAN TABLETS

The history of the collection of artifacts uncovered throughout the Midwest is very controversial and lengthy. Much has been written concerning these artifacts. The names they go by are "The Soper/Savage Collection," or "The Michigan Tablets" (Figure 7.1). To shed some light on these two names, one must understand who these people were, and what brought them to such an infamous end. I say infamous because most historical societies have dubbed them such.

During the summer of 1874, in Crystal, Michigan, a farmer was plowing his land and hit a large, flat stone. Stopping to move it out of his way he discovered it was not just any stone, but a highly polished piece of black slate. He examined it very carefully and could see that it had been engraved upon. The image of a man became visible on the stone after he wiped the dirt off it. The man in the carving was wearing a helmet. There was writing on the stone as well, which later was proved to be cuneiform.

It was during this same time that more and more artifacts began popping up in various mounds throughout the region, including all sorts of, knives, curiously designed boxes, stone tablets, and other interesting pieces. The mounds became fair game and they began to be torn down and excavated. Between 1858 and 1920, people from twenty-seven Michigan counties reported finding artifacts, most showing the same type of cuneiform writing.

No man helped to open more mounds in the Michigan area than did the Reverend James Savage, a pastor of the Roman Catholic Church in Detroit. He described the mounds:

> On these mounds you may find large and aged tree, oaks, pines, and other varieties. The decayed roots of pine and other trees that grew, thrived and died on these mounds are there. They contain another peculiarity. There is a stria (sic) of charcoal and ashes in each mound. This stria (sic) often shows the basin-shaped contour of the interior of the mound when its possessor was laid away to rest. There does not appear, as a rule, sufficient charcoal and ashes for cremation, only enough for purification. In some mounds, however, there is a heavy strata.
>
> These prehistoric mounds of Michigan contain caskets, lamps, bowls, pipes, tablets, etc. of clay: battle-axes, knives, spears, daggers, and arrow-points, domestic utensils, saws, chisels, spades, etc., and a variety of ornamental wearing apparel, all of chilled copper; stone tables, medallions, metals, skinning knives, various implements and of strange design, the object of which we can not imagine. One remarkable feature of these mounds, they contain no flint implements of any kind, nor have I seen any stone or copper beads; other ornamental wearing apparel is frequent.[1]

A man by the name of Daniel Soper, friend of Reverend Savage claimed to have personal knowledge of more than 3000 artifacts found throughout the area. Once the word "fraud" was heard around the finds, Soper was quick to defend the artifacts by saying, "If they are fakes and were buried to be found, whoever buried them has been a very busy person, because they have been found throughout the state by hundreds of different people."

He went on to say, "The objects recovered from the mounds are, variously, of copper, sandstone, limestone, burned clay and slate. The copper and slate objects predominate. The copper appears to be true mass lake copper. Of the slates the grayish black variety predominates, this being of the quality which outcrops near Baraga, in northern Michigan (Figure 7.2). The sandstone is of fine texture stone, now quarried at Amherst, in Ohio. Red and green slate limestone appears. These being of an argillaceous character and having a good polish."

Soper and Savage were strong supporters of the Michigan Tablets and together formed their opinion by the evidence they saw and gathered. They published their conclusions about the tablets but it brought nothing but a long series of criticisms. The learned men of the day could not, or would not concur with the two men's theory that the artifacts were from ancestors of modern Indians who arrived in North America; a race of white people with superior intelligence and culture who left their mark in prehistoric mounds throughout Michigan and the Ohio Valley. Of course it is well known how Major John Wesley Powell managed to bias minds of the scientific brains of the day. He was never in favor of a layman's report of an archeology find. As soon as he heard of one he would consider the report a fraud! Soper and Savage soon found that their lives were in ruin because of their stand on the Michigan Tablets. Their credibility had fallen from grace.

During the course of the next few years, many of the Michigan Tablets and artifacts found their way to the University of Notre Dame. Several of the other Michigan artifacts were dumped in trash pits or broken up as shooting targets for young men. Many of the tablets simply disappeared. Not much was heard about the collections until many years later.

It wasn't until April of 1960, when two young LDS missionaries by the names of James Bird and Paul Roundy paid a visit to Father Charles E. Sheedy at Notre Dame University, that interest in the collections began to resurface. The two missionaries had been assigned to the Indiana South Bend Mission, and Father Sheedy was in their assigned proselytizing area. Bird and Roundy were teaching Sheedy about their religion and related the story of the LDS prophet, Joseph Smith and his receiving the Book of Mormon records of the ancient Nephite nation, which were engraved on plates of gold and brass.

While engaged in their story, Father Sheedy interrupted them and commented that he had something to show the two young men. "I have some of the type of tablets that you are talking about," remarked Father Sheedy. This immediately aroused the curiosity of the two missionaries. Sheedy took the young duo to the attic of the university's O'Shaughnessy Building where he uncovered three crates. Out of one of the crates he removed several slate and copper tablets covered with hieroglyphics, pictographs, and strange inscriptions. This excited the two young men and they exclaimed to each other that here was proof that ancient people had indeed inhabited the continent. Bird and Roundy hoped that finding these tablets, and knowing that there was a connection with the story of the Book of Mormon, many people in the area would be converted. That was not how things turned out.

Father Sheedy did not want to be converted, nor did he want the missionaries to convert his faculty or student body. What he wanted was someone to either authenticate or disprove the value of the collection of tablets and artifacts. He thought perhaps the LDS Church could help in some way.

Not knowing what to do with their newfound knowledge, the young missionaries decided to let the matter rest with a higher authority. After they had returned to their apartment, the two wrote a letter to an LDS Church leader, Elder Milton R. Hunter, of the First Quorum of the Seventy. They never received a reply. What happened was nothing short of human error as Hunter had accidentally misplaced the letter. When he finally discovered what had happened, nearly two years had passed. He decided to write a letter to Father Sheedy at Notre Dame to ask for an appointment to visit him.

When Sheedy received Hunter's letter he was more than anxious to meet with the LDS General Authority. Hunter went to Notre Dame and examined the crates of artifacts. He was impressed to say the least. Unbeknownst to Hunter, Sheedy had already decided that the whole collection was going to be sent to LDS Church headquarters in Salt Lake City (Figure 7.3).

Some time later, while sitting in his office, Hunter received a message that some large crates had been unloaded at the train station. Confused and bewildered Hunter headed to the train depot to see what on earth had arrived in his name that would be in such mass. When he saw the return address on one of the crates, he was very excited. He had been given the Notre Dame collection of Michigan artifacts!

The complete story of the Soper/Savage story can be found in other publications. The reason for bringing this story to light is to suggest that the people who created these items, whoever they were, did a fair amount of mining in the northern parts of Michigan and nearby areas, for copper and other minerals. They also had gold and silver. The question is where did they obtain these precious metals? Who told them where to look for them? It is amazing that they had so much knowledge in so many different fields. Their tablets and artifacts prove that they were a sophisticated people, with great abilities.

The possibility that the tablets and other artifacts found in the Michigan mounds are frauds is remote. The find is too massive, too broad, and too perfect to be a fraud. The unearthed artifacts cover so many different states and have been found in areas that were not even subject to farming or building until the late 1800s or early 1900s. Why would someone plant artifacts where they might never be found? The answer is, they wouldn't!

The key to deciphering the Michigan Tablets and the other discovered artifacts may very well be accomplished by the "Ten Commandment Tablet," which came up missing from the collection housed at the LDS church Museum before it was sold to Professor Jon Halsey of the University of Michigan. With our knowledge of the Book of Genesis, we should be able to complete this task. The whereabouts of the valuable Ten Commandments piece is unknown, but the stone is preserved with photographs. Epigraphers are attempting to translate most of the Michigan Tablets as well as the Burrows Cave stones.

Figure 7.4 is a photograph of some of the Michigan Tablets when they were housed in the Church of Jesus Christ of Latter-day Saints Church History Museum.[2]

Notes

1. May, *This Land: Zarahemla and the Nephite Nation,* 20–49.
2. Shaffer, *Treasures of the Ancients,* 83–101.

CHAPTER VIII
ANCIENT SIGNS AND SYMBOLS OF THE AMERICAS

Much has been written about ancient cultures living on the North and South American continents. It seems everyone has their opinions and theories as to who these people were, where they came from, and where they went. We should keep in mind that the "proof" of such civilizations has indeed surfaced over the years, but certain mainstream professionals still scoff at these facts!

Books written by authors who never knew each other and were separated by cultures, time, and space seem to have collaborated on several key points in identifying ancient cultures of keen intellect and knowledge that inhabited both continents.

Mysteries of Ancient South America by Harold T. Wilkins is full of testimonials from many Native American Indians and early explorers who inhabited that part of the world telling of great cities and peoples who possessed technologies far beyond the capabilities of the day. *Tayos Gold* by Stan Hall gives detailed information about the Crespi Collection in Ecuador and the expeditions that tried to find the fabled "Cave of Gold"! And *Gold of the Gods* by Erich Von Däniken again narrates the testimonies of many people in regard to ancient white races of super intelligent people who inhabited South and Central America.

In addition, historians Wayne May, Fred Rydholm, Lyman Platt, the late Barry Fell, and Gloria Farley all contributed massive amounts of evidence pointing to a pre-Columbian inhabitation of our northern lands that can only boggle the mind!

Comparing signs and symbols between North and South America indicates that there was commerce between the two continents and that the peoples of each continent had knowledge of each other from the beginning.

Modern archaeologists and historians are beginning to revise their ideas on the antiquity of civilization in North and South America. Revolutionary discoveries in all parts of North and South America are becoming more frequent, such as the colossal stone head of a man found in the dense jungle of Mexico clearly portraying a highly civilized race of unknown age and origin. It was carved on basalt and was at least thirty miles from the nearest source of volcanic material. This colossal head looks like a European with strange inscriptions carved on the base of the stone. What's more, these same characters have been found on pottery and petroglyphic panels discovered throughout the North American Southwest!

Very strange petroglyphs from the Rio Negro Valley in Amazonas, Brazil have been discovered with men in rayed headdresses or crowned headdresses (Figure 8.1) wearing peculiar garments and holding strange-looking staffs (Figure 8.2).

Similar panels are found in Utah's Dry Fork Canyon northwest of Vernal, Utah, including the impressive "Three Kings" panel (Figure 8.3). Nearby this panel is a long line of more of the same types of figures drawn on the cliff faces at Sadie McConkie Ranch. Some of these figures appear to be of colossal size, suggesting there were giants in the land. Some explanation for the size of these figures may have come in 1875 in western Missouri when conical mounds, on high bluffs overlooking the Missouri

River, were opened to reveal skeletons with skulls of monstrous size! The lower jawbone of one of these skeletons was double the size of a modern man and its thighbone was huge, almost like that of a horse. The skeletons were found in a sitting position with weapons and tools laying on the ground around them.

Some of the hieroglyphic characters seen on panels in the Fillmore and Manti, Utah area shown in chapter two have been found in regions of South and Central America as well. And an additional discovery in the Dry Fork area, north of Vernal, Utah brought a new twist to our understanding of the ancient inhabitants of this land.

In 1988, a man by the name of Wayne Jones befriended a Ute Indian called Tom. Tom and Wayne became very good friends and during that time Tom took Wayne to a burial cave in eastern Utah where he was shown the remains of a giant man and a very large sword. Wayne was allowed to take the sword out of the cave for examination and dating (Figure 8.4).

Some time later, Tom became sick and died. At the funeral, Wayne brought the sword to give to Tom's family but they told Wayne it was the reason Tom had died: it was cursed and that he should take it back where it had come from immediately before he too met the same fate!

I heard about the sword myself from Ute friends and made contact with Wayne Jones. He told me that he had taken the sword back but it was too late for him—he claimed the curse was true and that he too was dying. I asked him where the sword was, to which he said, "You'll know when you see its sign."

A few years later I was conducting a tour in eastern Utah's Dry Fork Canyon at Sadie McConkie Ranch when I came upon one of the better-known petroglyph panels (considered to be Fremont). I had seen this panel a dozen or more times but never really looked at it until this day. There, plain as day, was the sign of the very sword Wayne Jones had told me I would find, attached to the back of this so called "Fremont Indian" in the drawing (Figure 8.5)! I realized that here, at Sadie McConkie Ranch, was where Tom and Wayne had removed the sword from the tomb! But because of the sanctity of this site and out of respect for both the landowner and the dead, I did not explore the matter further by looking for the cave or sword. We can only stand in amazement with mouth agape and wonder at it all.

The invading Spaniards knew only too well of the interconnection between the North and South American continents. They used this knowledge to plunder all they could out of the two without any conscience. First they pillaged Central and South America, then came north after finding there were riches to be had there as well. They used all their resources and gleaned information from slaves and bondsman to discover possible locations of past civilizations and treasure. Codes and symbology were used by the Spanish to keep secret the location of certain mines and treasures once they had found them! Some of these signs were those they had seen in Central and South America. Some of the signs and symbols they used had their true meanings changed to suit the great invaders so even their own countrymen would remain clueless about their hidden treasures! The Spanish trusted nobody, not even each other, so little tight-knit groups were formed and alliances made and oaths sworn! It was a terrible time for those on the outside because their lives meant very little to those of the Spanish "in" crowd!

Ancient Symbols

Many signs and symbols are not only found in South and Central America, but in the North American Southwest and represent only a small fraction of the hundreds of signs and symbols found in many regions throughout the world. The "pyramid" sign is found on a few of the hieroglyphic panels discussed in chapter two as is the "cross" sign. Both are found in China, Ecuador, and North America (Figure 8.8).

Note Figures 8.8 through 8.10 to observe symbols used anciently, as well as later by Spanish conquistadors. These symbols and inscriptions are found both in North America's southwest and South America's Amazon Basin.

CHAPTER IX
FATHER CARLOS CRESPI AND HIS FABULOUS TREASURES

The country of Ecuador has its share of secrets, ranging from age-old caves, tunnels, and temple artifacts, to ancient records hidden deep in the jungles of its interior.

A few hardy explorers have prospected for gold in the lowland Ecuadorian jungles bordering the dark Amazon. One such explorer was a man by the name of Juan Moricz, an Argentine citizen who, in 1969 loved to look for ancient mines and treasures of South America. He was an amateur archaeologist as well, with great interest in the cultures of the Amazon Basin and was credited with finding and mapping a network of underground tunnels stretching hundreds of miles south of Ecuador and Bolivia. Part of Moricz's report about his travels was a claim that he had uncovered an ancient and lost civilization previously unknown to the modern world.

Moricz had removed several fine artifacts from a cave in the eastern Cordilleras of Ecuador—a vast subterranean world containing a "metal library" and other fantastic treasures left there by an ancient civilization now lost to history. Since he knew he would be in serious trouble should the authorities find out, he petitioned the Ecuadorian government for legal custody of the artifacts. These objects included many stone and metal items of various sizes and colors. His requests, even to have a government scientist accompany him to the site, went ungranted.

Moricz had a friend who had contacts with the Church of Jesus Christ of Latter-day Saints (LDS Church), and it was through this friend that Professor Paul Cheesman from LDS Church-owned Brigham Young University (BYU) became involved in Moricz's project to document the artifacts of this ancient civilization. The LDS Church helped in many ways to acquire some of the artifacts for study. Many trips were made by several members of the First Presidency of the Church to make contact with Moricz, and more important, to meet the focus of the whole investigation, Father Carlos Crespi (Figure 9.1), the man who had the most knowledge about the cave and its ancient treasures.

Father Carlos Crespi was born in Legnano, Italy on May 29, 1891. Crespi began his life-long adventure when he was ordained in Verona at age twenty-six. Four years of continual study at the University of Padua, with a thesis in anthropology gave him a Master's degree that would be very helpful in the years to come. Crespi was somewhat of an over-achiever having collected additional degrees including doctorates in music, engineering, and the natural sciences.

In 1923, Crespi went to Ecuador, not as a missionary for the Catholic Church but as a scientist to gather information and artifacts for an International Missions Exposition to be held in Rome in 1925 and 1926. The poor people of Ecuador loved Crespi and trusted him. Because of this love and trust, many rewarded him with gifts of enormous value, which later became known as the Crespi Collection of ancient artifacts.

In 1969 the First Presidency of the LDS Church asked BYU professor Paul Cheesman, to follow up on claims that ancient Book of Mormon-type tablets and artifacts had recently been discovered in Ecuador. Cheesman, along with a few colleagues left

Salt Lake City in August of 1975 and flew to Ecuador for the purpose of interviewing Juan Moricz about Father Carlos Crespi and his knowledge of the ancient artifacts. Obtaining such an appointment was difficult but arranged through Moricz's attorney, Dr. Gerardo Peña.

In 1972, a man named Wendelle Stevens also became interested in the Crespi treasures. Stevens was in Ecuador on a totally different assignment looking for a wall painting that would give the location to a very vast Spanish treasure horde supposedly located somewhere in Ecuador. What he found instead, through Father Crespi, was a fortune in French and German paintings stolen from Europe during World War II by the Nazis. At a little cathedral, in shacks hidden behind it, were hundreds of these stolen paintings and artifacts that had allegedly been given to Father Crespi by the local Indians as tithing.

Even with all of the investigations on the Crespi Collection conducted by Paul Cheesman for the LDS Church and by Wendelle Stevens on his quest to find the treasure-map painting, Crespi never did reveal where the huge cave was located that housed hundreds more tablets and artifacts. While Juan Moricz claimed to have found the enormous cave with all its treasures, it was Father Crespi who knew exactly where the artifacts he guarded had come from and had the evidence to prove it!

Interest in the intriguing cave and documenting whatever treasures might be hidden in it did not rest solely with Juan Moricz, the LDS Church, or Wendelle Stevens. Barry Fell, an author and the founder of the Epigraphy Society had photographed much of the Crespi collection for future books and was very interested in the collection. In addition, another well-known American who had some knowledge of the cave was determined to find it. This man was none other than the world-renowned astronaut Neil Armstrong. Armstrong wrote Professor Gerardo Peña Matheus of Guayaquil, Ecuador; a government official of Great Britain; and some men with financial backing from Scotland asking to finance an expedition into the jungle to find this cave of the ancients.

Moricz was to act as guide in this expedition. Armstrong promised that all artifacts would be photographed, logged, tagged, and then left where they were found. After contracts had been signed and conditions accepted, it appeared all was ready to commence the expedition. However, there was a snag. The government of Great Britain made a major change in the contract, insisting that a co-expedition leader be named. Moricz and his attorney rejected the change but in spite of their objections, the British government determined to send another leader. They sent the director of the British Scientific Team, Dr. Philip Asmole. Just as things seemed to be working out, there was another blow to the plan. The British government decided they didn't need Moricz or his attorney because they already had news of the location of the cave and the underground treasures.

The new expedition, now led by Captain Peter Willis, was named "the Los Tayos Expedition." Neil Armstrong was a key member of the team. The group came in on a Royal Air Force cargo plane equipped with a great deal of scientific gear with which to explore underground tunnels. The expedition spent a number of weeks in the Ecuadorian jungles where they surveyed and mapped several miles of subterranean tunnels, but did not find the main chamber of artifacts and treasure. They found a few minor artifacts and a bit of gold here and there, but nothing worth a fortune as had originally been hoped for.

Once Moricz learned of the group's failure, he knew that his secret about the buried civilization was still safe. He figured that Neil Armstrong must have obtained his information about the cave's whereabouts from a man by the name of Erich Von Däniken, who had visited Father Crespi in Cuenca in 1973. Von Däniken had published a number of photographs of the Crespi antiquity collection. He even suggested that he was allowed to access the real treasures of Crespi's rooms in the College of Salesino, while others had only been shown one or two obscure artifacts from these rooms.

Von Däniken was not fond of Armstrong and had chided him

for his off-the-wall expedition. Armstrong replied to von Däniken in a letter dated February 24, 1977:

> *The Los Tayos Expedition, a joint project of the British and Ecuadorean governments, was formed to conduct a scientific study of the "caves of de Los Tayos." It is my understanding that the British Army was involved in some 400 such expeditions in 1976. Because of my Scottish ancestry, and the fact that the U. K. side of this project was largely Scottish, I was invited to act as honorary chairman of the expedition. I accepted. I visited the exploration site in early August this past summer. I had not read your books and did not know any connection that you might have had with the caves. I made no statements regarding any hypotheses you may have put forth.*
>
> *I understand that there have been magazine articles in Germany and Argentina which reported on the expedition and related it to your theories. Pictures were included which showed me at the site. I was not interviewed by representatives of either publication. I was asked in Ecuador whether I had observed any evidence of highly developed societies having been in the area, and I answered that I had not. I accept no responsibility for anything you may have read in the European press. I appreciate your kind invitation to join you in your forthcoming expedition, but I am unable to accept.*
>
> *(Signed) Neil A. Armstrong*[1]

The world of explorers did not believe Armstrong had failed in his expedition. They claimed that he did indeed make a significant recovery and somehow got it out of the country. Juan Moricz believed Armstrong would never compromise his position with the British Crown and was heard telling a colleague:

> How can someone stay underground for three days and nights, at a cost of more than $3,000,000 and walk away smiling? No, I don't believe they did not find something there. I do know this that they did not find the Library, but they will never do it without me to lead them. This

> expedition—with more than 60 scientists, army officers, proper equipment and the first thing they do is destroy an ancient altar. Who is guilty, for that? Myself, because I gave them the information about how to find the entrance! There was no gold down there, only stones and pottery! Can you imagine such as army with gold fever?

Besides creatures of the cave, the Neil Armstrong expedition made many archeological discoveries that were extracted from the Tayos Cave such as human bones, these important discoveries, the botanists that accompanied the expedition collected over 400 plant species with about 25 percent of them new to science. Several new species of bats and many species of butterflies and other insects were also discovered. The expedition might not have unearthed Moricz's "metal library" or statues of gold, but they did contribute a lot to science.

In 2001, twenty-five years after the Los Tayos Expedition, three men armed only with cameras headed high into the Andes Mountains of Ecuador to the peaceful city of Cuenca. Its red tile roofs and worn cobble streets mark the passage of ages gone by. The men knew where they were going and as they worked their way through the busy streets were greeted by native men wearing a single braid underneath "Pannama" hats and women dressed in earth-tone clothing with bright fringe. Many spoke to them in their native (vernacular) tongue. The men made their way to the College of Salesion. They knocked on an old wooden door of the college several times before it creaked open to reveal an inner courtroom. An old man led the trio to a private chamber where Father Carlos Crespi met them. The old priest recognized one of the men and extended his hand in friendship. That man, the leader of the group, was none other than the late Paul R. Brown, known as one of the world's leaders in ancient studies. The two others were Randy Johnston and Steve Young, both archaeologists. Brown was surprised that the old priest remembered him. But nevertheless he did.

Old Father Crespi led the men down an inner courtyard out to a wooden door where he pushed it open revealing a very stunning work of art from ages long since passed. At the end of this courtyard was a door, for which Father Crespi produced an old key that hung from his robe. He opened the door and with a helper disappeared into the dark room. They soon reappeared with a large piece of metal that had been molded and hammered into a long sheet. It was pure gold! The metal had curious looking inscriptions on it, and strange works of art. Crespi and his helper carried or dragged twenty-seven more pieces out of the room. Each new piece was impressive and more elegant than the last. All were gold, and all were very well constructed. Crespi told the trio that what they had just seen was only a small portion of what still lay hidden in caves of the ancients, under the silt debris. He would not reveal the whereabouts of the caves but would only say that someday a man would come that would carry the treasure out for the good of the people.

After Father Crespi passed away, the relics and artifacts were no longer available for public view and the sealed room was no longer open to those acquainted with Crespi. Crespi's entire collection was eventually shipped by the Catholic Church from Ecuador to Rome. The natives no longer brought artifacts to the Church and some even left the Church after Crespi died. The boxes of artifacts are now in the Vatican and confiscated as national treasures. Who will be the person to finally unearth the horde of golden artifacts that still lie in the jungle caves of Ecuador? Perhaps we will never know.

This story does not end here! In 2004, five people came to visit me at my home in Spanish Fork, Utah. Fletcher Richmond and Barbara Zuckerman, who at the time were friends from the well known "Sir Francis Bacon's Sages of the Seventh Seal" group, brought three other guests to visit with me. Those other three were Jason Gomes, Dari Plent, and none other than Wendelle Stevens, the man who had been in Ecuador around the same time the LDS Church was conducting searches for lost artifacts and had met Father Crespi in his search for a painting that would lead him to lost treasure. I had invited some other friends to attend this meeting as well. Randy Lewis, Wanda Price, John Labrum, and my wife Bonnie all were in attendance. Fletcher Richmond introduced us all around and then gave a brief overview of what was about to be shared with us. Wendelle Stevens began by giving us a slide presentation on the Crespi story about which I was very excited! I had always wanted to learn more concerning Crespi and the gold horde he had once guarded. I knew there was much more to the story than what I had learned previously.

Stevens began his presentation by showing dozens of color slides of gold and silver artifacts allegedly found in Ecuador and the surrounding area. He then gave us a background story that would tie the Father Crespi artifacts with him and another adventurer, Lee Elders. The two had gone to Ecuador in 1972 in search of an important painting that would lead them to the Kinara Treasure that had been lost in the Kinara Desert of Ecuador after a major battle between two sons of the great Inca Emperor, Huina Capac. Emperor Capac had divided his vast empire between his two sons, Huascaran and Atahualpa, Huascaran receiving the southern part with its capitol at Cuzco, and Atahualpa receiving the northern part with its capitol at Quito. However, as with most

spoiled children, one or the other wants what the other has and will attempt to acquire it at any and all costs! Atahualpa sought to take control of the empire for himself. He took his forces and marched south to meet his brother and there conquer him and his army and then loot their vast treasure there. However, the tide turned on Atahualpa and soon it was he that was being pursued. His brother Huascaran caught him in the Kinara Desert where they fought a fierce and bloody battle.

Atahualpa saw that he was about to go down in defeat and had to abandon the vast treasure he had looted at Cuzco. The forty or so animal-pack-train loaded with the treasure was unloaded and the treasure buried in the middle of a corral where the animals were held. The animals trampled the burial site all night long leaving no trace of a major dig. By the time the battle had reached its bloody climax, Atahualpa and his beaten forces had to abandon the treasure site for fear of death by the army of Huascaran.

Upon hearing the intriguing tale of Atahualpa and his brother, Stevens and Elders were determined to find the lost loot, so they began researching and interviewing everyone they could, which led them on a quest to find an old Spanish painting that supposedly contained clues as to the whereabouts of the Kinara Treasure. As they continued their research, they eventually met an old Indian living on a land-grant who directed the pair to an old church that bore a painting of an artist's rendition of the battle on the Kinara Desert. The painting hung in a local parish church on another old land-grant belonging to an aristocratic family. That family no longer lived on the land but had moved to Cuenca, and in their place the head of the Central Bank of Ecuador resided. This man's name was Osvaldo Rendon, who remembered seeing the painting hanging in the family church on the land-grant property when he was a boy. Another old Indian servant living on the property told Elders and Stevens that the church had been closed when the family moved away. The local priest packed all the church property, including paintings and fixtures and took them to Cuenca. Stevens and Elders went off to find this priest at the headquarters of the Saliciano Order in Cuenca.

Osvaldo was enlisted to act as guide for the pair. He agreed to take the two to the headquarters of the Saliciano Church to see what they could find. He said he knew the old priest in charge and could get them in. He further explained to them that he had seen many old paintings there. The collection had never been open to the public, but he had been given permission to visit there because his aunt's estate had removed some of her things to the tiny Saliciano Church.

Rendon, Stevens, and Elders finally made it to the church. They met the priest at the door. He was a spry old man who claimed to be about eighty-seven years old. He stood firm and his posture was erect. His eyes were deep blue and his hair long with a balding top. He had a flowing gray beard. His robes were frayed at the hem and his shoes were worn out. His sleeves were so frayed that they had been turned inside out at least a couple of times and sewn over and over again. He was a true member of the poverty order of Catholic Priests, the Salicianos, who deny themselves even the most minimal living comforts. He slept on a straw mat and had but one blanket. His meager meals consisted of hard, dry grains and a small, hard bread called "pancitas." The old, poor priest was none other than Father Carlos Crespi.

Stevens continued his story by telling us that Rendon asked Crespi if he wouldn't mind showing the group some of the paintings he had seen at the church when his aunt's estate was there. The old priest agreed, and then led them down a narrow corridor to an inner court, up a flight of stairs and around a balcony where he opened a locked wooden door. Inside were some very fine paintings, their subjects in pain and sorrow over the plight of their Christ. The Kinara Desert painting they were seeking was not among the many there. Rendon said that he remembered an old shed where paintings were kept and asked Crespi if they could see them as well. The old priest hesitated but finally agreed to show the paintings, first explaining that the group was not allowed to follow him to the old shed.

After a short while Crespi returned from the shed with several Spanish Colonial paintings somewhat similar to those found in the little land-grant church. The painting Stevens and Elders wanted was not among these. Crespi shrugged, picked up the roll of paintings to return them when Rendon said, "Here, let me carry those for you," and he took them from Crespi. He followed the priest back to the shed. Soon Rendon and Crespi returned with more paintings, this time with some Flemish and Venetian works.

Crespi again went to the shed and returned with another armload of paintings and laid them out on a table. There were three Spanish Colonials featuring an old man in a robe, a shepherd boy with a cross, and a person's portrait on glass. The priest seemed to be quite proud of some of the paintings, almost as though he were showing them off. He picked up the painting of the shepherd boy with the cross (Figure 9.4) and said, "This was one of Raphael's first works, done in 1506 when he was twenty years old." He pointed to the portrait on glass and said, "This is interesting because it is one of only two such paintings known, both painted in reverse on the back of the glass by Tiziano [Titian]." Another painting on a slab of translucent sandy-orange marble had to be viewed with backlighting like a stained glass window. Another painting of the bust of a hairless old man with a brown robe over his shoulder still had an engraved label on the back.

Rendon, becoming disenchanted by their distraction with other paintings again said, "What about the paintings from the old church on my aunt's property?" Crespi left the paintings on the table and went back for more. While waiting for the priest to return, one of the men picked up the old man portrait and turned it over. It had a paper label on the back with French writing on it: "Property of the Muse Gran Montrouge, Paris." A number was branded in the wooden stretcher. Some of the other paintings had markings indicating European ownership or origin. This caused the men's eyebrows to rise.

Crespi came back with more paintings on their original wooden stretchers, but none with frames. Here were more of the same. As he gently laid them down on the table, Rendon could see that none were from the land-grant church. When Crespi began to gather up the earlier paintings he had brought out, Rendon offered to help him once again. The other men followed behind and soon were led to an old wooden lean-to shed against a perimeter wall. As they went inside they could see that there was no lighting inside the shed, so one of the men raised his camera and shot one flash of what looked like a huge freestanding board bookshelf packed with paintings on their wooden stretchers. The paintings had no frames. Some were stacked in piles on the wood floor, and even more were rolled up, having been cut free of their stretchers.

Crespi was shocked by the camera's flash and turned quickly to shoo the men out the door. He was very protective of the contents of that little shack. Some time later Stevens returned alone to visit with the old priest. He soon gained his trust and was allowed access to the paintings, which numbered in the hundreds. Stevens began taking coffee table art books on his visits with Crespi, which the old man enjoyed very much.

Rendon agreed to see what he could find out about the origin of all those paintings. He came back with evidence now confirming their suspicions that the local Indians did not give the old priest the paintings as tithing as they had been led to believe previously. Upon questioning some of the natives, Rendon learned that the old priest had come into possession of the paintings quite by accident! It seems that he was the superior of a missionary whose parish was a small jungle village on the east side of the Andes Mountains, about six miles from the southern coast of Ecuador. Crespi had seen a foreign man driving an English four-wheel drive Overland truck arrive at a small village about six miles in from the southern coast of Ecuador sometime in late 1943. Whatever cargo the man had loaded was under a canvas covering the back of the truck. This man bought a building site on the edge of town and positioned the truck on it. He then hired carpenters and specialists and built a house around the truck, where he lived alone for many years. He never left his property for more than a few hours, and always had it within his view. He never brought anyone home with him. He accepted the local missionary parish priest of the Saliciano Order of the Catholic Church as a friend with whom he could converse on profound subjects, and who helped him perfect his Spanish, since initially he had a strong German accent.

The German, in time, lost his accent and blended into the local society to the extent that many regarded him as one of their own, and forgot his mysterious arrival.

A time came when the man fell ill and the Saliciano Priest treated his friend as best he could. The man worsened and the priest finally diagnosed his illness as cancer and told him he would have to go see a specialist. But the man refused to go anywhere away from his home. His cancer advanced and before his end he summoned the priest for Last Rites. In his last days, the German penned a will leaving his home and all its mysterious contents to the Saliciano Order of the Catholic Church.

Not long after the German was buried, his priest friend visited the home along with a trusted assistant to inventory the goods for the church. As they walked over the wooden floor it sounded hollow in certain places so they removed some boards to see what was under them. There they found several wooden crates filled with paintings—well over a thousand of them. They had been cut from their frames and some had even been cut from their stretchers. The priest notified the Saliciano headquarters in Cuenca and they arranged to move the paintings to Cuenca, where they were housed in the wooden shed under the care of Father Crespi.

Stevens reported that while getting a hamburger in Ecuador as he waited for a plane, the proprietress of the restaurant he was eating at, an American widow by the name of Betty Mann, came over to talk to him. Her husband had been a German mining engineer in the employ of the Ecuadorian government. He had passed away from a fatal heart attack leaving her alone, so she opened a hamburger shop as a means to support herself. Stevens enjoyed talking to the woman because they both spoke English. During the course of their conversation Stevens mentioned the paintings he had seen and the story of how Father Crespi came into possession of them. This led her to tell Stevens a story that she said might have some bearing on the subject.

Betty Mann told Stevens that sometime during 1943 a foreigner with a German accent contacted her husband, the owner of a small yacht in Guayaquil harbor, to charter it to go deep-sea fishing. Mann tried to refer him to one of the other fishing boats that regularly took visitors deep-sea fishing, but the German was very persistent and wanted to go out alone. He kept offering Mann more money until Mann could no longer afford to turn him down, and thus agreed on a day that they would set out for the open sea.

The German and Betty Mann's husband sailed out of Guayaquil harbor early in the morning, in the direction of the Galapagos Islands. The German produced an ocean chart of the area, which he had marked with the coordinates of where he wanted to fish.

Upon arriving at the spot he ordered Mann to put out the anchor and to get the fishing gear ready. Before they were ready with their gear, a black conning tower rose out of the water alongside them and they were suddenly looking at a German submarine.

The conning hatch tower opened and a man appeared. He called over to the German on Mann's boat, who replied in German. Soon more men appeared on the deck of the submarine and began opening the end of a large black cylinder. They unscrewed many big wing-nuts on the canister and then removed the end. Other German sailors produced an inflatable rubber raft. This raft was put over the side and sizable wooden crates were pulled out of the cylinder and loaded onto the raft. It was then moved over to the yacht where Mann was instructed to lift the crates aboard with his deck hoist.

Once the crates had been loaded on board, one of the sailors boarded the yacht. Mann's passenger produced another map and instructed Mann to sail to a sandy cove in deeper water on the south coast of Ecuador.

Arriving there about 4:00 p.m., the Germans put the rubber raft back into the water and lowered the boxes into it a couple at a time and took them to shore. When the operation was complete the German ordered Mann back to Guayaquil.

On the way back, Mann advised the German that he had just involved him in a smuggling operation, and that he would have to report the German. His passenger said he didn't believe Mann would do it, because he would be gone, and the boxes would be gone, and the only party to the action left would be Mann, leaving the Ecuadorian authorities no one to investigate but Mann himself.

Mann discussed the incident with Betty, but the couple

decided to do nothing and that was the way it was left right up until Mann's death. Stevens was the only person she had ever told the story, and said that if asked later about it she would have to deny it.

Stevens found out that the paintings were not all that Father Crespi was sitting on in Cuenca. He had more lean-to sheds against that perimeter wall, and more storerooms full of art and art objects. Eventually Stevens was allowed by Father Crespi to view the items in these rooms. One room contained a corner with a pyramid of stacked stone heads, from floor to ceiling with a base about five feet out from the corner, like those seen in the Kalua liquor advertisements. These heads were valued at about $100,000 to $300,000 each. Also in this room were carved stone ménages, carved figures of humans, and animals and abject shapes that fitted together into one composite stele. Stevens found the objects interesting, realizing they were rare enough that few others had probably ever seen them. One item that Stevens inspected came apart into four separate carved figures, all blending into one when assembled. There were stone eve coping blocks that ran in a line obviously from some kind of a temple or palace. There were carved panel blocks in stone, matching the coping blocks but these were much bigger and had stylized heads and designs that might have been decorative wall panels below the coping blocks.

One room Stevens entered was filled entirely with Tikis—giant black eight-foot-tall totem figures carved in guayacan, a wood so dense and hard that it will not float, and is used for maritime dock pilings because even barnacles will not attach to it. This room also contained a canoe covered with silver plate. Crespi had a pottery room as well, filled with all sizes and kinds of pottery, from small cooking pots to very large storage pots, big enough to hold a child, or even a man. Some were elaborately decorated while others were not. There were other pottery utensils such as serving dishes and bowls, and even musical instruments like whistles, flutes, and accordions.

Crespi had a gold room as well! It was filled with gold objects of all kinds including statues, sun discs, vases, pots and plates, and even creatures, such as a small alligator, that were both modeled in gold and covered with gold leaf. Many of the objects had been recovered from caves and old temple ruins in Father Crespi's parish area. At Paiute, a highway crew cutting a new right-of-way for a future road accidentally discovered one such cave sanctuary. Their bulldozer blade cutting away the shoulder of a hill opened a hole in the side of the cut. They could see that it was a cave of some sort. A man was sent in to investigate. He did not come back out so another man was sent in to get him. That man did not come out either so a priest was sent for. The Saliciano missionary priest recognized the problem and instructed the men to make another hole and ventilate the cave for a day. They did this and the priest himself went in to retrieve the two lost men.

As he entered the cave, he was surprised to find himself in a treasure sanctuary belonging to some long-lost civilization of the past. He saw a number of giant Tikis carved in guayacan. He saw big clay pots and some storage bottles of clay. Under many inches—nearly a foot deep in some spots—of bat guano, the priest found solid gold tablets averaging some eight to twelve inches long, by six to nine inches wide, cast in deep relief, up to three fourths of an inch thick, in gold-bar form.

These plaques appeared to be sand castings that had been rubbed out to a fine, shiny finish on one side, probably with guayacan sticks to give them almost a jeweler's finish on the front. The backs had a gold finish but not dressed to improve them, and one half by two and a half pegs molded into them, apparently for mounting them to a wall. These golden plates weighed thirty to fifty pounds each depending on their size.

Some of the plates, both in gold and silver, had cleaved gemstones of ruby, sapphire, and emerald pinched into small cavities made in the metal. The scenes depicted on these plates seemed to represent an unknown civilization—probably, Stevens thought—of Pacific Island origin. The style and arrangement

Figure 1.1: Utah's own ancient astronaut (left: close up).

Figure 1.2: A rising five-sided star with radiant beams on the sandstone mound panel near Hanksville, Utah.

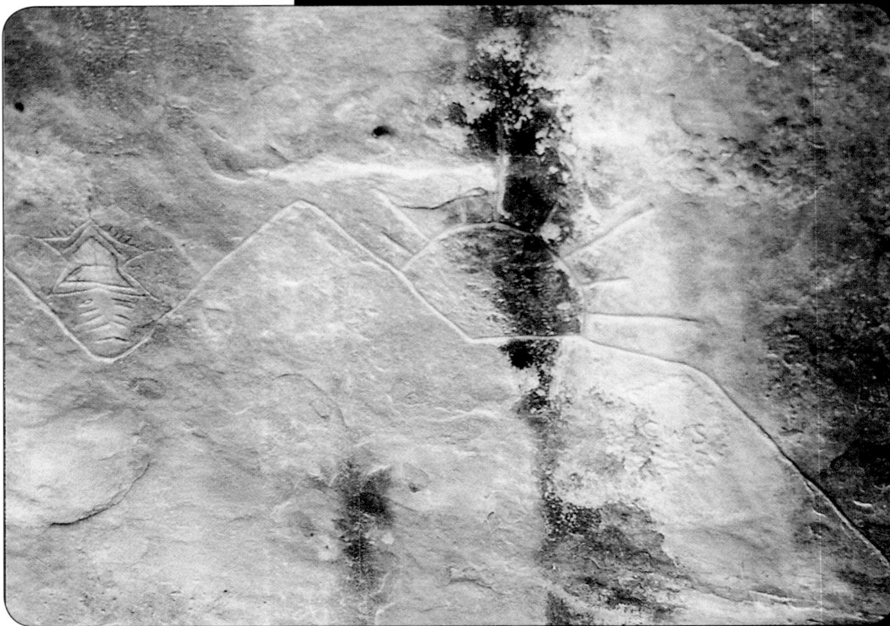

Figure 1.3: The rising sun with the star at far left on the panel at the sandstone mound, near Hanksville, Utah. Smaller symbols not visible in this photograph.

Figure 1.4: Two stone teepees, one barely visible at the right, on the sandstone mound panel near Hanksville, Utah.

Figure 1.5: A ghostly face appears from the rocks twenty meters from the main sandstone mound panel near Hanksville.

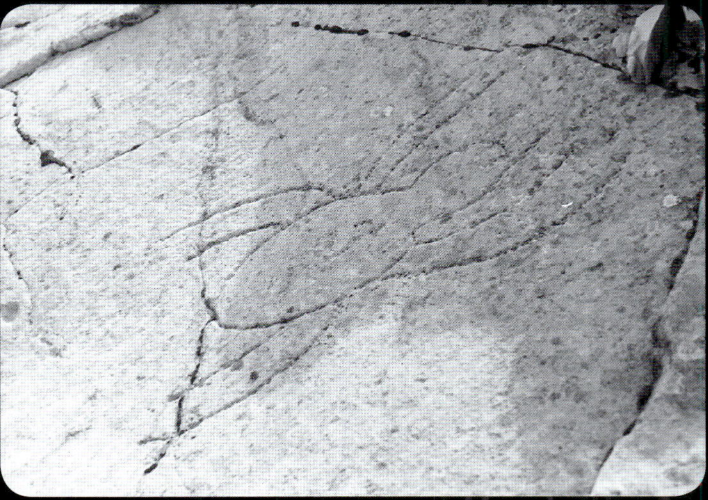

Figure 1.6: A giant five-foot spider high on a 45° granite wall, east of the main sandstone mound panel.

Figure 1.7: Strange bird-like glyph with sun cross at its beak, near the main sandstone mound panel, Hanksville.

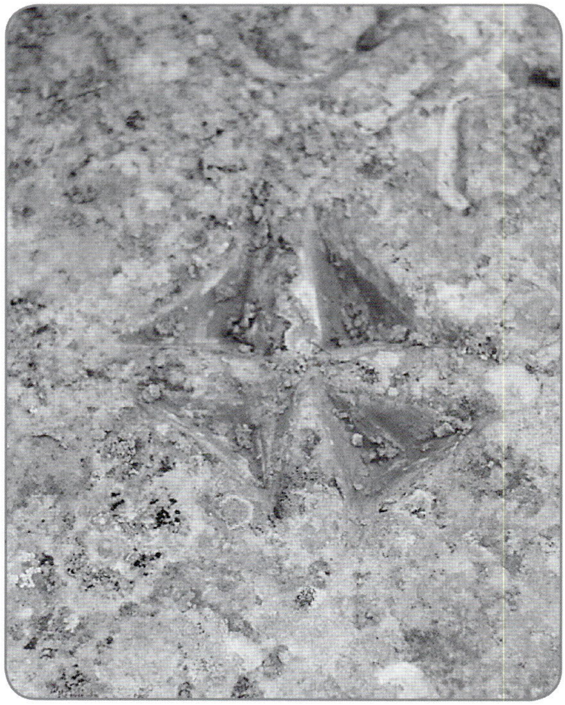

Figure 1.8: The Malta Cross on the sandstone mound panel.

Figure 1.9: This sign was used by the Spanish to denote church treasure.

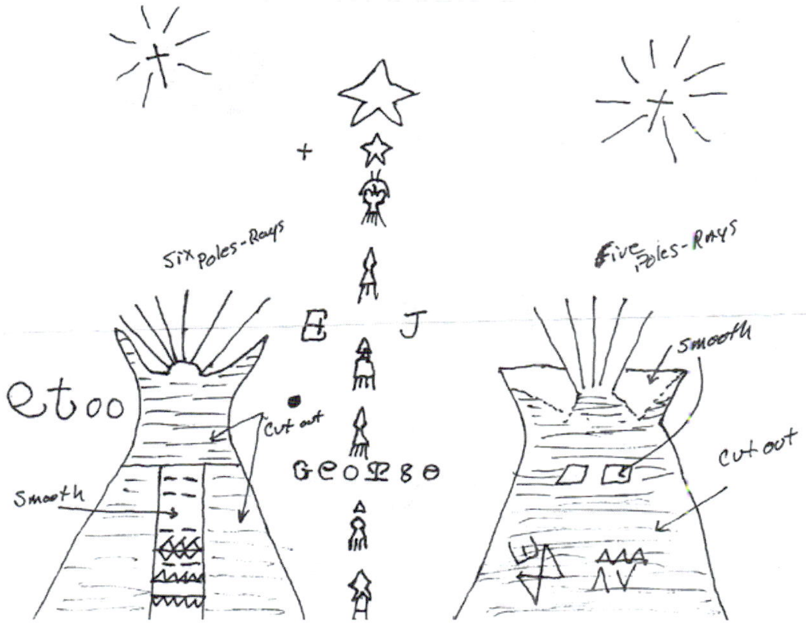

Figure 1.10: Hand sketch of the panel at Cottonwood Canyon by Danny Marshall of Spanish Fork, Utah.

Figure 1.11: Ancient language strangely depicting space travel on a panel near Blanding, Utah.

Figure 2.1: Commonly known as "The Shot Put Man" this man in relief has been the subject of controversy as to when it was carved at this site near Cedar City, Utah. Testing indicates 200-plus years ago.

Figure 2.2: An impressive hieroglyphic panel half a mile north of The Shot Put Man.

Figure 2.3: Vandals have all but destroyed this ancient panel behind the Manti Temple of the Church of Jesus Christ of Latter-day Saints in Manti, Utah.

Figure 2.4: Second set of hieroglyphic inscriptions north of those pictured in Figure 2.3.

Figure 2.5: Witches Knoll has produced evidence that humans constructed it from earth pulled from a canyon one mile east.

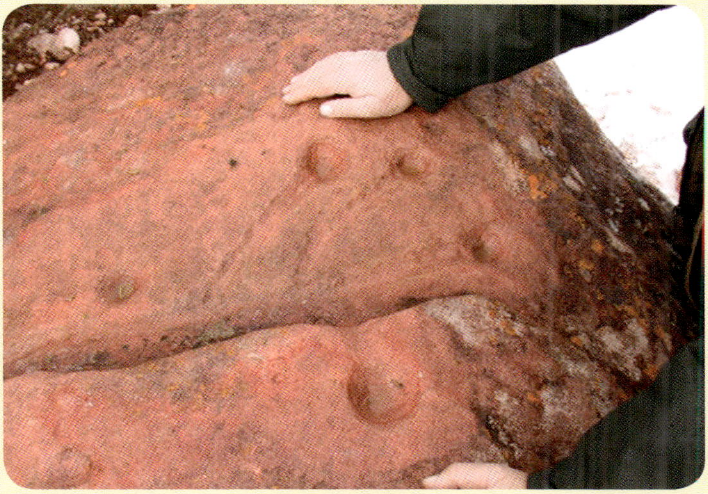

Figure 2.6: The "map rock" at Chalk Creek, east of Fillmore, Utah.

Figure 3.1: Chalk Creek hieroglyphic panel.

Figure 3.2: The Signature Rock at Chalk Creek, Fillmore, Utah.

Figure 3.3: (above) Frank Beckwith at a Linotype machine (1948).

Figure 3.4: Beckwith photo of "Signature" glyph inside ochre-colored hand on Signature Rock, 1941.

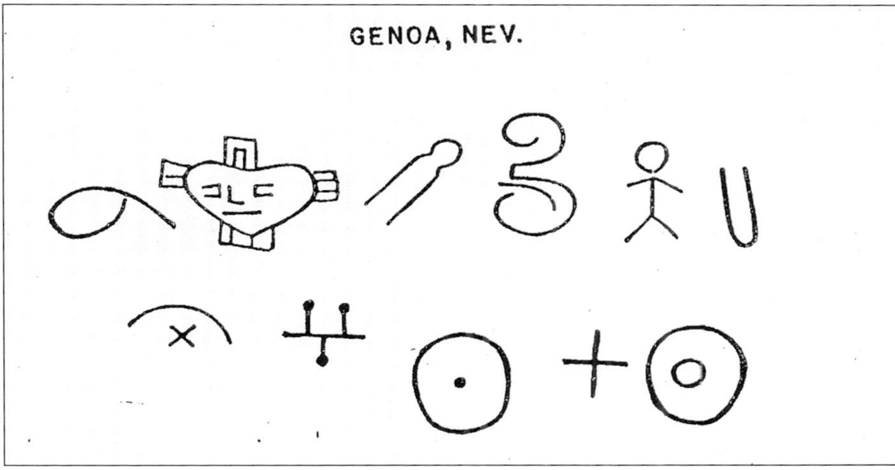

Figure 3.5: Hieroglyphic panel at Genoa, Nevada.

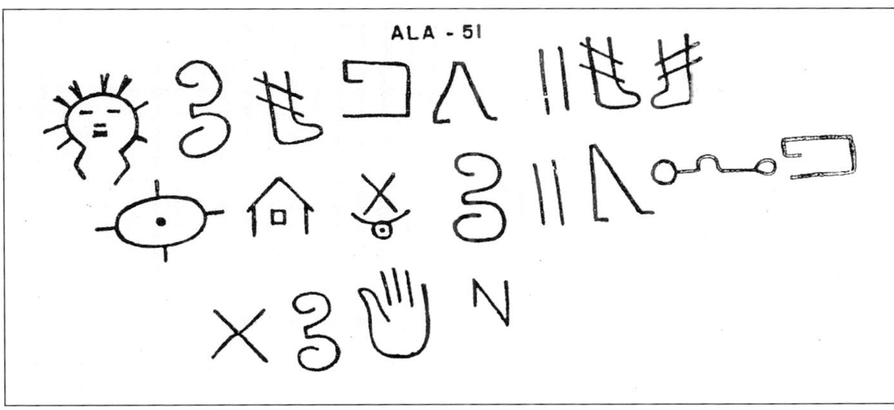

Figure 3.6: ALA-51 Panel.

Figure 3.7: SOL-16 hieroglyphic located in California.

Figure 3.8: Roman lead crosses with Latin inscriptions found at Tucson, Arizona.

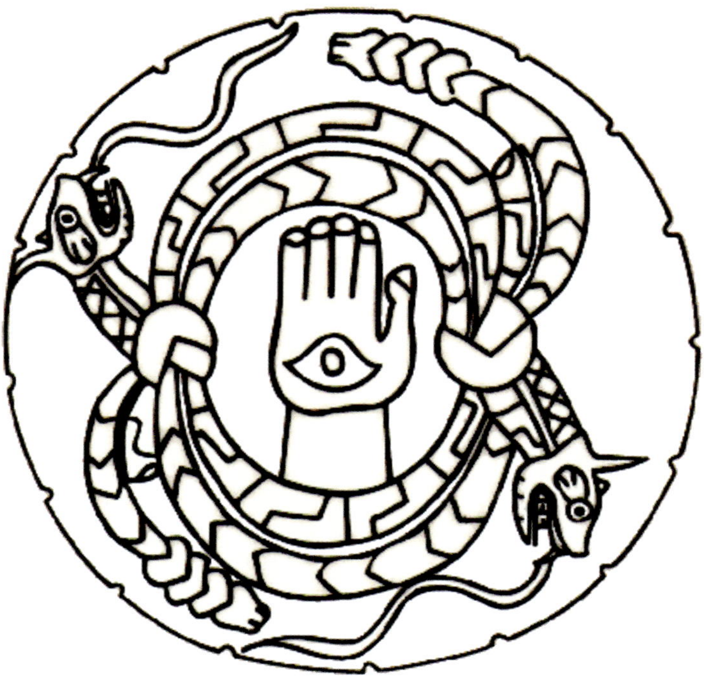

Figure 3.9: Mudras discovered at Moundville, Alabama.

Figure 3.10: The eye inside the hand at Chalk Creek.

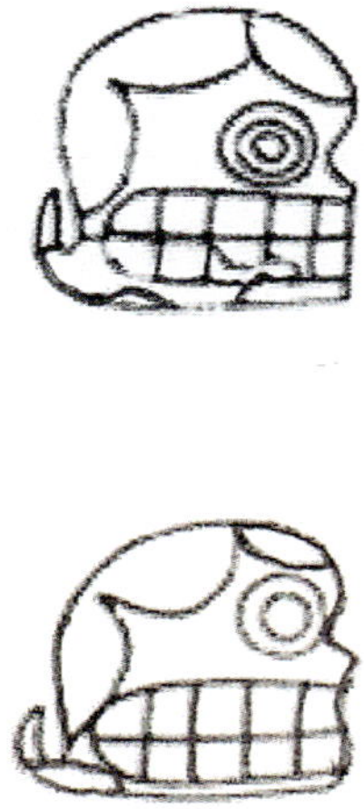

Figure 3.11: Typical skull drawings found on pottery at Moundville, Alabama.

Figure 3.12: This panel was discovered in Kentucky. Note the similarities between its inscriptions and those of the panels in Figures 2.3, 2.4, 3.13, and 3.14. (Photo courtesy of *Ancient American Magazine*.)

Figure 3.13: This hieroglyphic panel is situated southeast of Nephi, Utah on a high cliff. Access is limited to those in shape to make the hike.

Figure 3.14: A hieroglyphic panel in New Mexico similar to the Utah panels with small differences.

Figure 4.1: Eugene Aagard at his home in Levan, Utah with lamp.

Figure 4.2: Lamp discovered south of Price, Utah by Aagard.

Figure 4.3: Lamp of marble construction.

Figure 4.4: Part of the Manti Collection of artifacts owned by the family of the late John Brewer of Sanpete County, Utah.

Figure 4.5: Samples of the metal tablets taken from Brewer's Cave.

Figure 4.6: Stone box shown above is from the John Brewer Cave in Sanpete Valley, Utah. The bark is still attached to the outside with metal plates showing.

Figure 4.7: Other artifacts with ancient script found in Brewer's Cave.

Figure 4.8: Copper artifact with inscription of a man's head, found in Brewer's Cave.

Figure 5.1: It is obvious the placement of this twenty-ton boulder at Fish Lake, Utah, is not an act of nature.

Figure 5.2: These photos are examples of the dolmen-style monuments found in the Sanpete Valley of central Utah. Note the Patriarchal cross (or double cross) symbol carved into the bottom right dolmen.

Figure 5.3: Two of America's largest dolmens dating to circa 2500 BC when Old Norse and northwestern Europeans penetrated northeastern America.

Figure 5.4: A six-foot structure with "pointer" near Fish Lake.

Figure 6.1: A marble tomb stone depicting a person of great importance, discovered by Russell Burrows.

Figure 6.2: Author Steve Shaffer and *Ancient American Magazine* Editor/Publisher Wayne May, with a Burrows Cave "portrait stone."

Figure 6.3: Gold coins and bars found in Burrows Cave. Burrows had many of them melted down and sold for money.

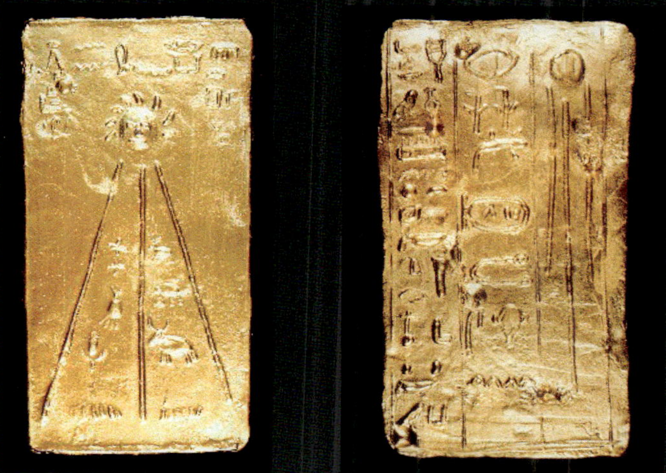

Figure 6.3: A lesser king or ruler, found by Russell Burrows in the cave.

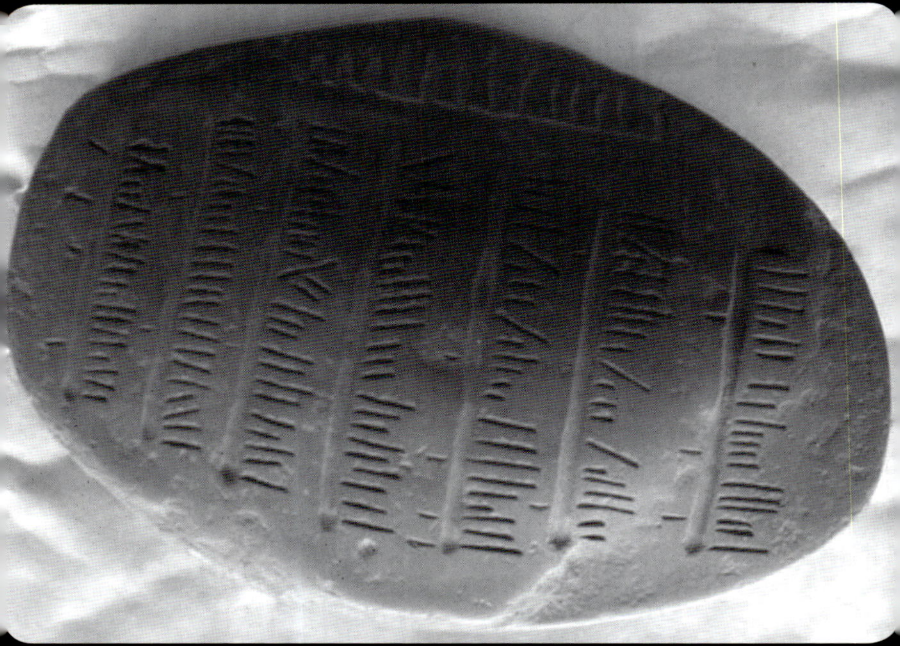

Figure 6.4: Burrows cave stone in Ogam Script.

Figure 6.5: The Crucified Christ (above).

Figure 6.6: Examples of the styles of black stone artifacts that have come from the cave.

Figure 6.7: Examples of Burrows Cave stones.

Figure 7.1: The famous "Ten Commandment Tablet" made from copper.

Figure 7.2: A black slate box that was dislodged from the roots of a 200-year-old tree in Michigan.

Figure 7.3: The author, Steve Shaffer, with the Michigan collection of tablets and artifacts at LDS Museum warehouse in Salt Lake City, Utah.

Figure 7.4: Copper tablets with two types of script etched into them.

Figure 7.5: (above) Another view of the black slate box found in Michigan.

Figure 7.6: (right) Engraved tablet depicting the Tower of Babel. From the Michigan collection.

Figure 7.7: (below) Soles from shoes, from the Michigan collection.

Figure 7.8: Assortments of tools from the Michigan collection.

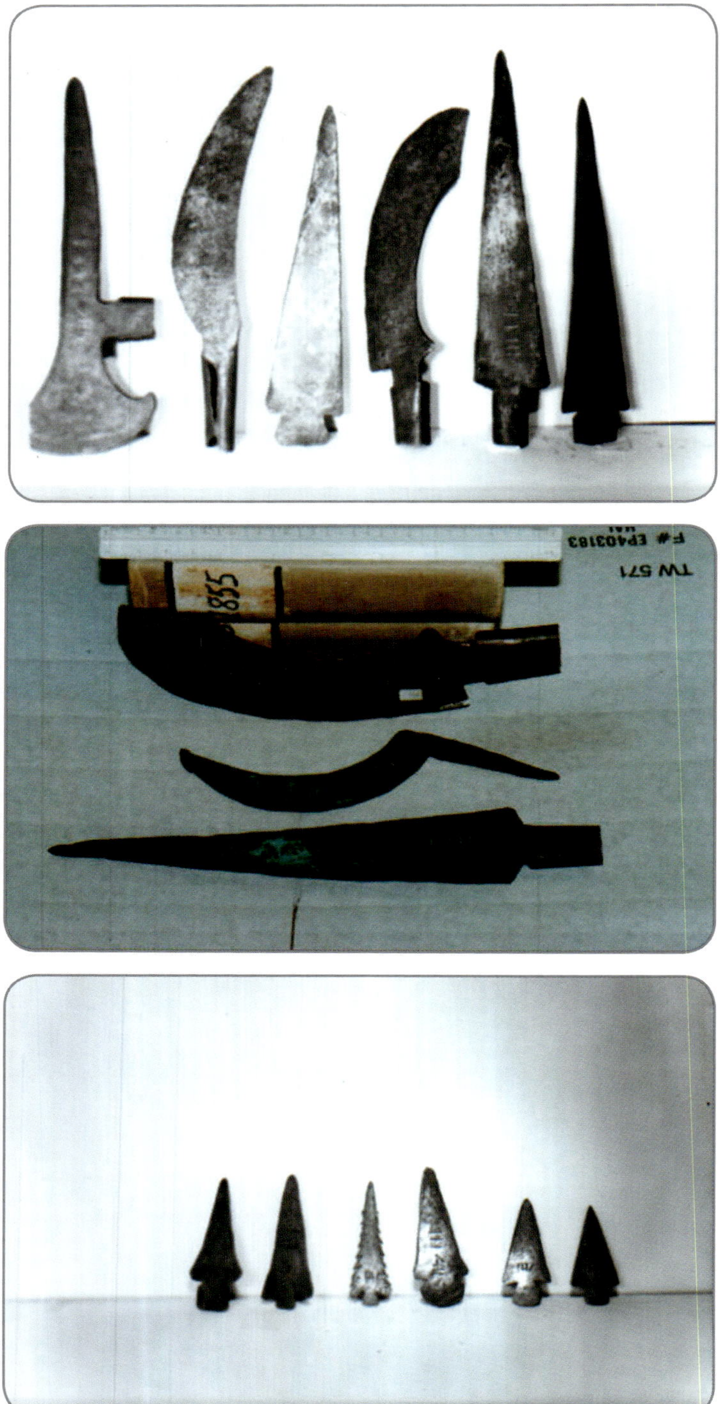

Figure 8.1: Typical headdresses worn by high priests of ancient South America.

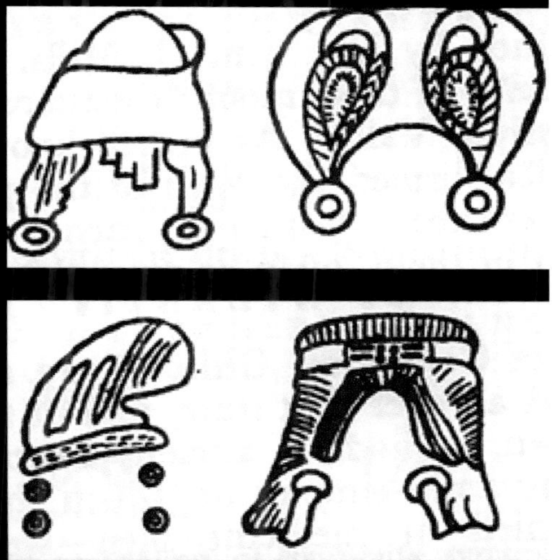

Figure 8.2: Men in rayed headdress, suggestive of priests, from a petroglyphic panel in Rio Negro Valley, Brazil.

Figure 8.3: Known as the "Three Kings" panel, this carving stands sentinel over a large array of similar petroglyphs in the Vernal, Utah, area. Some in the academic community suggest that the characters represent the "Fremont Culture," circa AD 650-750.

Figure 8.4: The large, Roman-looking sword removed by Wayne Jones from the Ute burial cave at Sadie McConkie Ranch in Vernal, Utah.

Figure 8.5: "Big Foot," as this panel is called, gives us reason to believe the people here depicted was a race of Libyans that came exploring the Green River drainage in southeastern Utah. These large petroglyphs without explanatory inscriptions seem to depict a warrior people. Note the sword on the back of "Big Foot"; could this be depicting the same sword that Wayne Jones discovered (Figure 8.4)?

Figure 8.6: A lone guardian stands watch over the roaring waters of the Green River in Eastern Utah.

Figure 8.7: This strange map was allegedly discovered by an Apache named "Apache Jim" in northern Arizona. The inscriptions shown have not been deciphered.

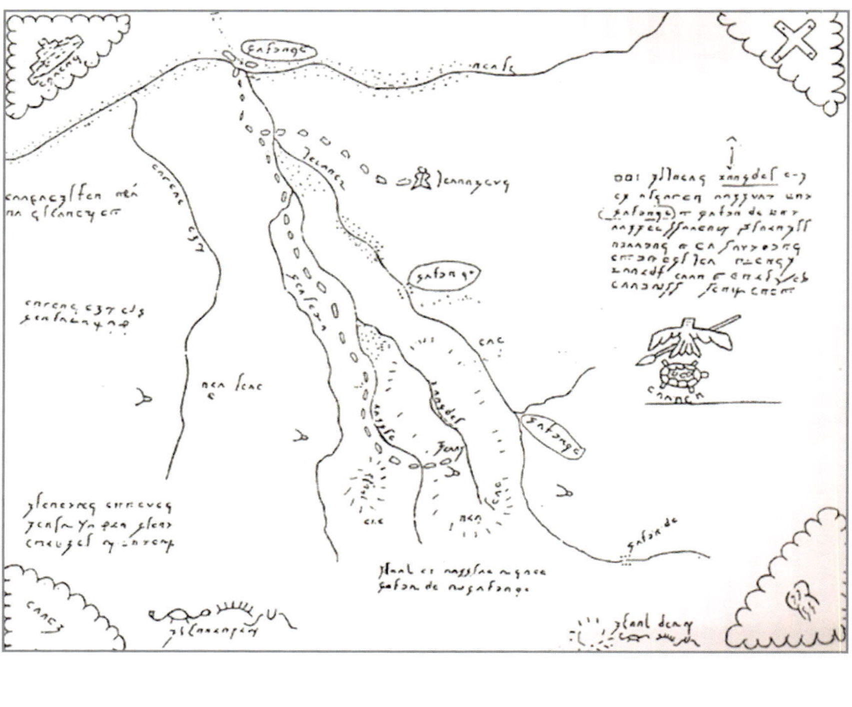

Figure 8.10: Similar signs and symbols are found throughout the southwestern States.

Stricken in years

Hy-Brazilian

Earth and Heaven

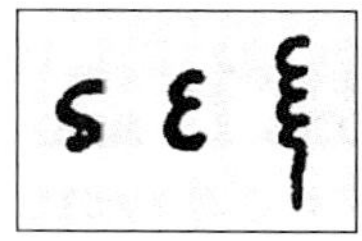

Renewal

Cross

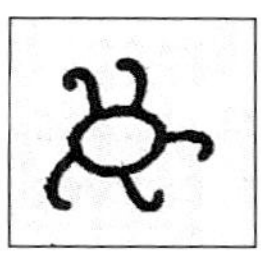

Swastika

Pyramid

Very old woman

House/ China

House/ Brazil

House/ Mexico

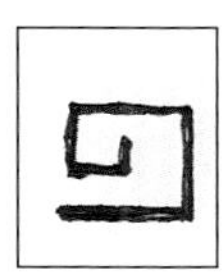

House/ Egyptian

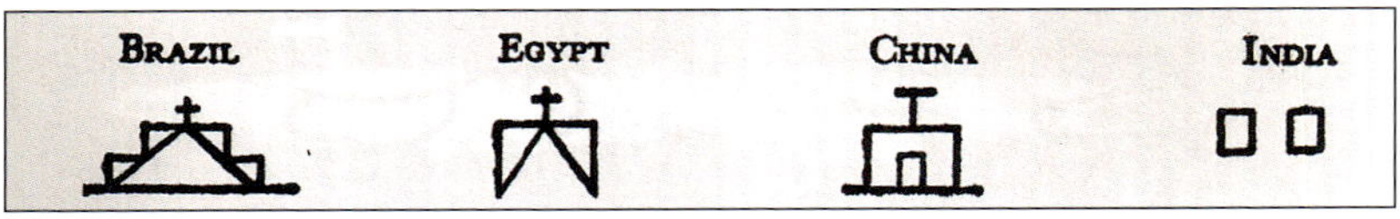

Figure 8.11: The following symbols were used anciently and later by Spanish conquistadores. These symbols and inscriptions are found both in North America's southwest and South America's Amazon Basin. These symbols shown on trees were used by the Spanish circa 1700- 1800.

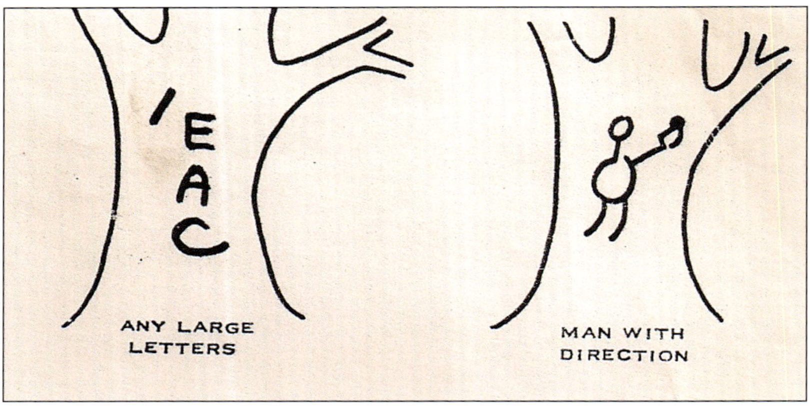

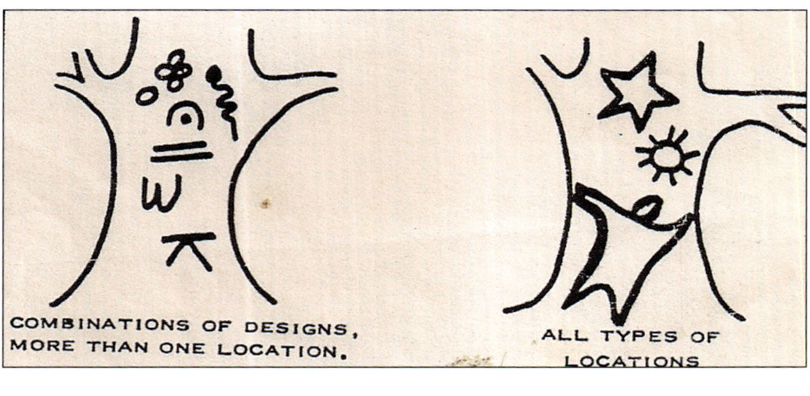

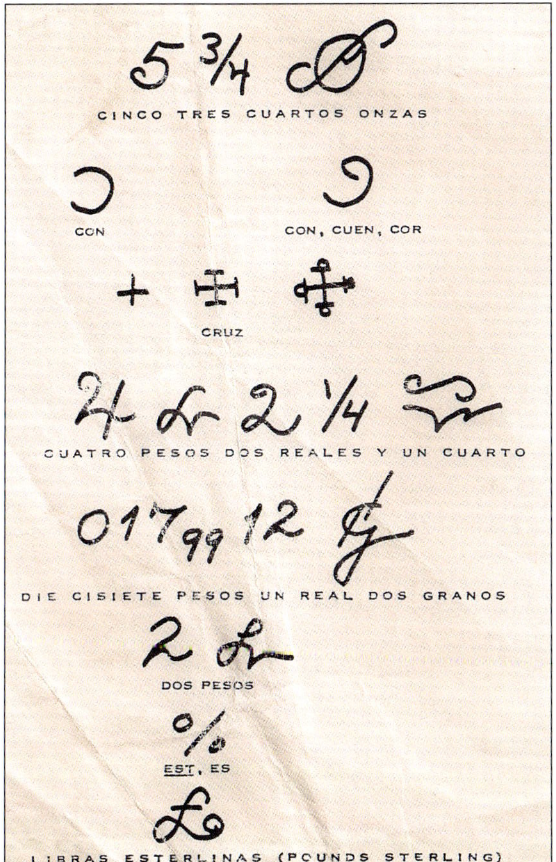

Figure 8.12: These inscriptions were used by an array of cultures and adopted by the Spanish to use in New Spain during their time searching for and collecting mineral wealth, circa 1500–1800.

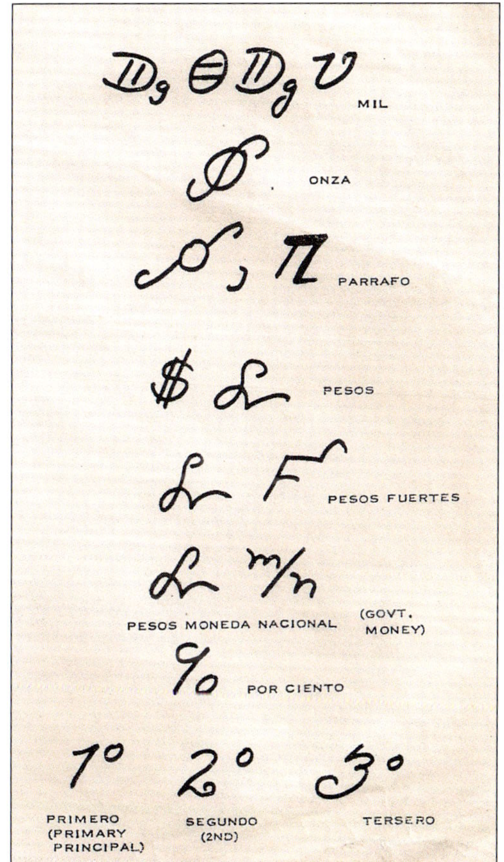

Figure 9.1: (left) Father Carlos Crespi Croci, the guardian of the sacred records.

Figure 9.2: (right) Crespi with Wendelle and Bonnie Stevens.

Figure 9.3: Crespi and Osvaldo in stone room.

Figure 9.4: Raphael's "Shepherd Boy" circa 1506.

Figure 9.5: A solid gold tablet of a high priest or holy man; part of the Crespi Collection.

Figure 9.6: Wendelle and Bonnie Stevens examine an ancient golden artifact shown to them by Father Crespi.

Figure 9.7: These three objects from the collection depict astronomers of different cultures and races, with the idea that clutching the serpent means mastery over his enemies.

Figure 9.8: (left) A solid gold dore, Pacifica, as named by Crespi.

Figure 9.9: A fine specimen of a sand cast metal tablet portraying a Syrian or Phoenician astrologer-priest. Inscriptions date to circa 1100 BC. One of the finer objects in the Crespi Collection.

Figure 9.10: Solid silver dore casts. Crespi Collection.

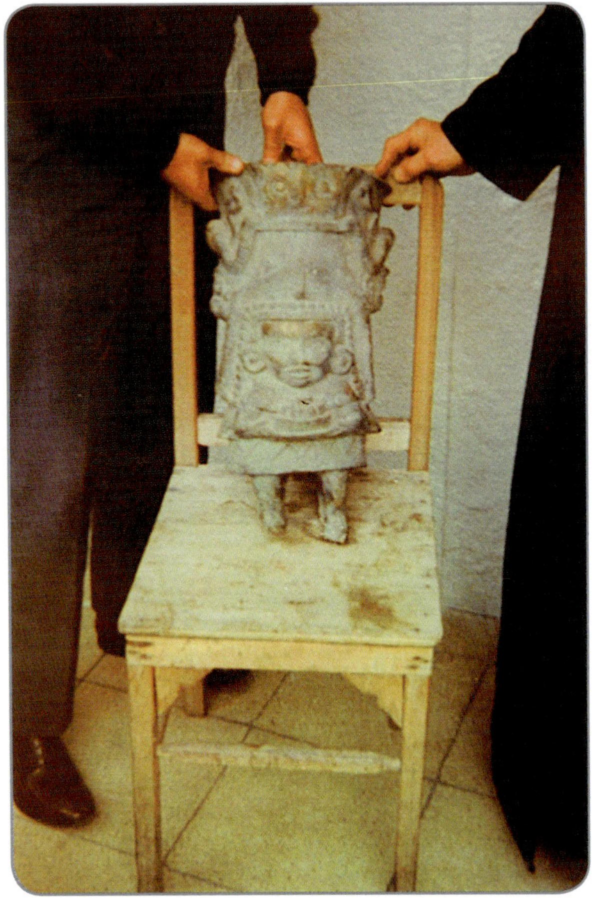

Figure 9.11: (left) The artifact on the chair was part of the Father Crespi collection and was said to be so heavy that it actually broke the legs of that very chair. It took three Indians to haul the edifice into the outer chamber for viewing. It is hollow inside, but made of pure gold.

Figure 9.12: Stevens holding up a stone statue.

Figure 9.13: (right) These two artifacts claimed as part of the Crespi collection have been dubbed fakes. However, there is no proof of this.

Figure 9.14: Gold artifact from Crespi's collection.

Figure 9.15: (left) Bonnie, Wendelle, and Osvaldo being shown artwork by Crespi.

Figure 9.16: Solid silver sand casting from Crespi's collection.

of the furniture, garments worn, and hairdos displayed on the human figures, did not fit any known society. There were also symbols and designs in the floors which did not match any symbols Stevens had ever seen before. "They did not fit Assyrian, Babylonian, Etruscan, Hittite, Sumerian or any of the Middle Eastern cultures," Stevens told us. One plaque had a temple scene with a priest at an altar and a tile floor of squares. Each square had a different symbol on it.

While showing the paintings, Crespi took Stevens and Bonnie, his wife, out back of the mission to a row of rundown old shacks. At the door of the largest shack was where they stopped. Crespi took a key out from under his long flowing rob and inserted it into a large round lock and turned it. The door squeaked open. Crespi pushed his way into the inky darkness. Somehow he found a lamp and lit it. The glowing flame cast eeriness about the room—almost supernatural in nature. He moved to a shutter covering a window a few feet away and set the lamp down. He then pulled a rope hanging there, and revealed the light of the summer's day. What Stevens and Bonnie beheld took their breath away! All about them stood statues, plaques, and strange edifices made from what looked like gold and silver! Crespi smiled then began to give them the grand tour! Stevens beheld a treasure horde that cannot be matched anywhere in the western world. The photos are only a handful of the massive treasure that Crespi was steward over (Figures 9.2–9.16).

The array of artifacts was over-powering and caused Stevens to stand and stare as if in a trance! Literally hundreds of gold artifacts lay hidden in the depths of this old shanty. It had been filled by the natives of the region, who continued to bring new artifacts to Crespi on a continual basis. It seemed that not a year went by that something new was not brought to the shanty.

Stevens was told by Father Crespi that there were huge caves in the jungle that went for hundreds of miles in several directions. Ancient cultures had hidden their treasures deep inside these caves. In one such cave hundreds of gold tablets were discovered by guano harvesters. Two feet down in the slime, laying on the bottom of the limestone cave, some 200 gold tablets and figurines were uncovered. How they found their way to the caves is anyone's guess. However, it is assumed that they were stolen from their owners and hidden there by robbers for safe-keeping. It is highly unlikely the owners or artisans of these fine pieces would have hidden them there. But we can't know for sure.

The late Stanley Hall, (see chapter ten) explorer and author, gives us a look inside this lost world of ancient South America through the testimony of Petronio Jaramillor, a native of Ecuador. Jaramillor was not shy and never hesitated in giving Hall all the information of his discovery. He still remembered the adventure into the Tayos Cave or one of its tributaries as if it were yesterday.

In 1946 when Jaramillor was just seventeen years old, he made the pilgrimage to the cave by following instructions from an uncle who had raised him. Apparently this uncle had been shown the cave by local Indians of the region because he was trusted.

The description of the contents of the cave is astounding! What this young lad saw is the envy of every explorer on earth! To give the reader but a taste of what was seen, I will relate a small portion of Jaramillor's account:

> Then all of a sudden, an overwhelming sight appeared before me, unbelievable in my widest imaginings. Entire libraries, full of heavy voluminous books! Moving over to one of the books I glanced through one or two pages of opaque, yellow metal. They seemed to be written by a single person, in a near perfect script, similar to modern taquigraphy; in low-relief, the impression on the other side of the page confirming the script was stamped one side only. Also there were known symbols—crosses, circles, semi-circles, squares, triangles, stars.[2]

He went on to tell of thousands of volumes of golden books

in the library and more. It seemed to him there had to have been thousands of years of continual placement of artifacts in the cave, which he described as colossal, with over ten separate rooms or caves!

Stanley Hall passed away never being able to see this vast horde he most earnestly sought! How many people have searched for it is unknown. It still lays hidden in the remote jungle of Ecuador, secreted away and protected by the jungle, swampland, animals, and tribes of Indians that would just as soon kill a man as to let him enter the great grave of the ancestors of the old world.

Many scholars have ventured into Ecuador in search of answers to their questions about the age of mankind and for religious awakenings. Some have gone there to prove their theory that ancient inhabitants came from that part of the world and migrated to northeastern North America to become what some believe were the ancient Hopewell Culture or Nephites of the LDS Book of Mormon. For whatever their reason, these explorers went to Ecuador, but most came back dissatisfied with little to show for it.

One thing this collection does imply is that anciently, people covered much of both North and South America in great numbers long before recorded modern history suggests. Evidence found on both continents tells a different story than what modern historians paint for us. As seen in previous chapters, many different cultures came and went but left us with hints of their being here. All across North America we find new evidence of great migrations, mining, farming, settlements, and commerce. Mainstream academia must open its eyes and admit its error in advocating modern history as acurate!

Anciently originating petroglyphs reveal to us the magnitude of this migration of nations to South America but as shown in previous chapters was not an isolated instance!

Notes

1. Courtesy of Kelly, Dan, and Gordon Nielson.
2. Personal papers of Naconna Barlow Shaffer.

CHAPTER X
THE LANGUAGE OF NUMBERS IN CODE

THIS FINAL CHAPTER HAS BEEN INCLUDED AT THE END OF THE book for those who wish to search out biblical codes. These biblical codes were widely used by early Spanish explorers and others who wanted to secretly transmit and receive information to and from their peers and colleagues. It would be wise to purchase an OSO Bible or "Biblia del Oso" translated into Spanish in AD 1280 to aid with understanding the symbols and numbers presented in his chapter. Words and phrases differ greatly from the modern King James version of the Bible, and the OSO can be a great way to learn the language of numbers.

Many groups used language in association with numbers: the Spaniards searching for gold and silver, the Jesuits, the Knights of the Golden Circle, and the Knights Templar's hiding up their untold wealth. It should be noted here that this usage differed from one group to another but in essence the usage of this system was constant.

The language of numbers was, in the beginning, associated with biblical passages and was used primarily to simplify written passages from the Bible. The language of numbers changed with the coming of groups to the Americas either searching for or hiding up treasures of all types and descriptions. These groups, including the ones mentioned above, came with riches and control or domination over the lands and the people and did not want competition of any sort. Codes had to be created to protect their wealth and loot. Since the Bible was the book of choice in those times, it seemed only fitting that the language of numbers be used to benefit those in control. This meant of course that the true meanings of the verses in the Bible would have to change. And change they did, ever so slightly, but they did change!

Every passage from the Bible used on maps or documents by the Spanish had an alternative meaning. Take for example the following passage from II Esdras 4:36-37:

"He has weighted the world in the balance, and has measured the times with a measure, and carefully counted the hours, and he will not move or disturb them until the prescribed measure is reached."

From this passage, it is therefore understandable that along with the architectural perfection of the physical creation, the Lord of Hosts has also numbered the times and seasons, as stated by the Prophet Esdras.

Using this same passage we can use the meaning for a different purpose. "He" could mean the viceroy or the king. Such a person is in total control. It could be said that the king or viceroy would be the one who could and would control the time when something, someone, or an event was to take place. The language from this verse could be considered a code in any sense.

The measures of chronology come from the Bible, the Great Pyramid of Giza in Egypt, and from significant constants in astronomy, mathematics, and the world of nature.

Lunar, Mean, and Solar Time

The sun, moon, and stars were appointed "for signs, and for seasons, and for days, and years" (Gen. 1: 14). From time to time calendars have been based upon the moon, upon the sun, and upon both in combination. For hundreds of years, Western nations have used a calendar based upon the solar year of 365.24 days, but the Jewish and Mohammedan peoples still employ one based upon the lunar year of 355 days.

There was also in use among the ancients an intercalated calendar year of 360 days. This is the Prophetic Year of the Scriptures, with each month being the twelfth part of it, or thirty days.

Divine time-cycles may be applied upon any or all of these three scales: the lunar year, the solar year, or the 360-day calendar year which is the average of the other two.

As a simple example, take 1,260 days, which is exactly 3??½ prophetic years or 3??½ times 360. But 3??½ solar years would be 1,278 days, while 3?? ½ lunar years would be only 1,242 days.

3½ Lunar Years = 1,242 days
3½ Prophetic Years = 1,260 days
3½ Solar Years = 1,278 days

Solar values for all prophetic periods may be calculated upon the following formula in which the number 666 is used as an example:

360 : 365.2424 : 666 : X

Solving this proportion by multiplying the two inner terms (365.2424 × 666), and dividing the result by the remaining term (360), will show the solar value of 666 to be 675.7. In actual application, it may appear as 675 or 676 days.

Since the lunar year is not a fixed value, varying about a mean length of 354.36 days, it is not possible to calculate the lunar values of prophetic periods quite so precisely as the solar. For the shorter time-measures, the value 355 may be used as a basis for calculations, that being the actual length of the lunar year in practice. For the longer cycles, the date marking the lunar termination will be found by subtracting from the mean value the difference between the solar and mean values of the cycle.

The following table gives lunar, mean, and solar values for the more common time-measures:

Lunar	Mean	Solar
282	286	290
414	420	426
656.3	666	675.7
828	840	852
1025	1040	1055
1241.7	1260	1278.3
1271.2	1290	1308.8
1315.6	1335	1354.4
1576.7	1600	1623.3
1862.5	1890	1917.5
2483.4	2520	2556.6

It should be noted that a different set of values pertains when the time-cycles measure a span of lunar or solar year, as they do upon occasion. In the case of lunar years, 1,260 years is equivalent to 1,222??½ solar years; 2,300 lunar years is equal to 2,231½ solar years, and so on. These shorter values are common when the time-measures are applied in years, but are found infrequently in day-to-day chronology.

On **lunar** time, dating from a given event of the past, we arrive at a terminal dating on which a related event will occur, but it will be seen by the watcher as in the moonlight; not clear, not distinct, nevertheless, outlined as by the light of the moon, giving just a general idea of its shape and form.

Applying the **mean** time measure from the same given event in the past, the terminal date will give a clearer conception of what may be expected when day fully comes; for this is the breaking of the dawn when that which was seen under the moonlight is disclosed in more detail, although not clear-cut, not fully defined, yet seen as by the light of the sun not yet fully risen.

Finally, **solar** time from the given date expires when the predicted developments already indicated—as in the moonlight, and seen somewhat more plainly, as at daybreak—are now clearly revealed, as in the light of the sun at high noon. Thus, all three scales of prophetic time periods, by which terminal datings are obtained, guide the watchers in their comprehension of the times and seasons.

The Numbers

Numbers associated with words, phrases, codes, and so on, are used today as much as they were thousands of years ago. However, meanings and usages have changed with some of the numbers in association with languages. This is how the Jesuit or the Spanish Crown would use numbers and languages to aid in perpetuating riches from the New World. This is also true with the KGC (Knights of the Golden Circle), Knights Templar, and Free Masons.

An explanation of the meaning and use of individual numbers is as follows:

(1) There can be no doubt concerning the significance of this primary number. The number 1 is the symbol of *unity.* As a cardinal number, it denotes unity; as an ordinal number, it denotes *primacy.* Unity being indivisible, it is independent of all others, and it is the source of all others. Catholic priests once used it to signify "Deity" or the "First" words of the Bible: "In the beginning was God."

(2) The number 2 is associated with the Incarnation—God, the Son, the Second Person of the Trinity. Two affirms that there is a difference—there is another. Two can be had for that which is "good" or that which is "evil." It was used at times to mean: "At the mouth of two witnesses", or "double witness."

(3) In this number we come to a new set of phenomena with the first geometrical figure. Two straight lines cannot enclose any space; three straight lines are necessary to form a plane figure; and three dimensions of length, breadth and height are necessary to form a solid figure. Three, therefore, stands for that which is solid, real, substantial, complete, and entire. In addition to this we can see in the scriptures that three becomes divine and marks divine completeness and perfection. God's attributes are three: omniscience, omnipresence, and omnipotence. Three is the number associated with the Godhead, for there are three persons in the Godhead. The number 3 is also second in the series of prime (indivisible) numbers. Three was used commonly among the Jesuits and the Spanish Crown to denote worthy sites, mines, treasures, or missions.

(4) The number 4 has reference to all that is created; it is emphatically the number of creation. It is the number of things that have a beginning, of things that are made, of material things, and matter itself. It is the number of material completeness. Hence, it is the world number, and especially the "city" number.

(5) This number signifies *grace* or *favor,* which is truly divine in its source and character. The believers of the time indicated the following: "We have the Three Persons of the God head and their manifestation in creation. Redemption follows creation because, in consequence of the fall of man into sin, creation came under a curse. Thus we have: Father, Son, Holy Spirit, Creation and Redemption." These are then the five great mysteries and five, therefore, is the number of grace! Grace means *favor* but what kind of favor? Favor to the unworthy is called grace! Five is also the third in the series of prime (indivisible) numbers. Thus, it partakes of the significance of both numbers involved (5 and 3).

(6) This is the number that indicates *imperfection*—the human number! It is the number of man as destitute of God; without God; without Christ. It is 5 plus 1, the grace of God made of none effect by man's addition to it. Or, it is 7 minus 1; man's coming short of spiritual perfection. In any case, therefore, it has to do with man. Six is also the number for *labor.*

(7) The first natural division of time is stamped by the number 7. On the seventh day God rested from His work of creation. Seven is a holy number; a number of spiritual perfection. It is the fourth in the series of prime (indivisible) numbers. Seven was used to denote that which is "*holy*" and "*right.*"

(8) Resurrection is the great fact that is signified by the number 8. It is also associated with *regeneration*, *renewal,* and the beginning of a new era or order! Eight is the dominical number, for everywhere it has to do with our Lord Jesus Christ. When written in threes (888), it is the numerical value of the name "Jesus" in Greek.

(9) In mathematical science, the number 9 possesses properties and powers which are found in no other number. It is the last of the single digits, marking the end, and is significant of the conclusion of a matter. Nine is, therefore, the number of finality or judgment. It is a factor of 666 (9 × 740). Nine was used by the Spanish on certain treasure signs, intending it to mean "The End."

(10) This number means "completeness of order." Marking the entire round of anything is the ever-present signification of the number 10. It implies that nothing is wanting; that the number and order are perfect; that the whole cycle is complete. Ten is one of the perfect numbers and denotes ordinal perfection. It signifies the perfection of divine order, commencing, as it does, an altogether new series of numbers.

(11) There is not much about the number 11 in the scriptures, but what there is denotes it to be significant, especially as a factor. While 10 is the number of perfection in the divine and non-divine order of things, this number marks disorder, disorganization, imperfection and disintegration. This number was used by Jesuits and Knights Templar alike to warn others. It has even been seen on Spanish panels where mines and treasures were depicted.

(12) Here again we have a perfect number. This number signifies governmental perfection (if one can believe that!). It is found as a multiple in all that has to do with rule. Twelve is the product of 3 (the perfect divine and heavenly number) and 4 (the number of material completeness on earth). Twelve is 3 multiplied by 4 and denotes that which can scarcely be explained in words, but which spiritual perception can at once appreciate, such as organization—the products denoting production, multiplication, and increase of all that is contained in the two numbers separately. The 4 is generally prominently seen in the 12.

(13) This factor has a widespread reputation as a number of ill omens. The key to its significance is given in Genesis 14:4, where we read: "Twelve years they served Chedorlaomer, and in the thirteenth year they rebelled." Hence the number 13, and its multiples stand for "rebellion, apostasy, defection, corruption, disintegration, revolution", or some kindred idea. Now if this number is in combination with the number 8, then it signifies "Atonement." Thus, the two numbers, 8 and 13, are like two threads—gold and crimson—which run through the whole divine revelation, continually crossing and re-crossing each other.

(14) Because 14 is a multiple of 7, it partakes of the significance of 7. Being a double, this number implies a double measure of spiritual perfection. The number 2, with which it is combined (2 × 7), brings its own significance into the meaning since 2 is the number associated with incarnation.

(15) Because 15 is a multiple of 5, it partakes of the significance of 5 and also of the number 3, with which it is combined (3 × 5). Five is the number of grace and 3 is the number of divine perfection. Therefore, 15 refers especially to acts wrought by the energy of Divine Grace. In chronologic reckoning, 15 is an hour: in a day of 360 degrees, 15 degrees to an hour; in a year, 15 days to an hour; in time, 15 years to an hour.

(17) This number stands out very prominently as seventh in the series of prime (indivisible) numbers; thus, it partakes of and intensifies the significance of the number 7. Indeed, it is the sum of two perfect numbers—7 and 10—7 being the number of spiritual perfection and 10 of ordinal perfection. Combining them together this creates the perfection of spiritual order.

(19) This number is the lunar, or Metonic Cycle at the end of which, in years, the moon repeats its phase. It is also a combination of 10 and 9 and denotes the perfection of Divine Order connected with *judgment.* It is extremely interesting that this number is eighth in the series of prime (indivisible) numbers and therefore partakes of the significance of the number 8.

(20) This number was used extensively by the order of the Jesuits. It is a double 10 and may in some cases signify its concentrated meaning. Owing to the Biblical application of 20 years, as a period of waiting, it is established that, primarily, this number is that of *expectancy.*

(21) This number is threefold and signifies divine completion (3) in regard to spiritual perfection (7). It is one of many perfect numbers. It is also the number of intercession (Dan. 10: 2 & 13).

(22) This number indicates "intensified form, disorganization and disintegration" but is mostly known for its significance from the fact that it was the length of Jacob's troubles.

(23) This is the ninth prime, or indivisible number (1, 3, 5, 7, 11, 13, 17, 19, and 23). Being the ninth in the series, it partakes of the significance of the number 9, which is "*finality*" or "*judgment*." Now, there is more to this number. It was used anciently as well as in modern times for similar things. In *Webster's New International Dictionary* it tells us that 23 means: (1) in railway telegraphy, a signal to signify a message of the greatest urgency. (2) A number signifying the end or completion; a command to go or move away; as, he said, "23, so I had to skip—or 23-skidoo!"

(24) This number being a multiple of 12 (12 + 12 = 24), it expresses, in a higher form, the same signification. It is the number associated with the heavenly government and worship, of which the early form in Israel was only a copy. It was so with the 24 courses of priests in the earthly temple; these were formed on the "pattern of things in the heavens."

(25) Always means *grace* and has the significance of 5 whether used alone or occurring as a factor in larger numbers.

(26) This number is the cube of 3 (9 × 3 = 27) and partakes of the significance of both 3 and 9.

(28) This number is the product of 4 times 7 (4 × 7 = 28) and partakes of the significance of both 4 and 7. Interestingly it is associated with the "Aubrey Hole." [28—that is, on the axis of the Aubrey Circle (of 56 holes) at Stonehenge]—has a relationship to the powers of prediction, to "celestial cycles" and the understanding of heavenly things. Also, 28 × 90 equals 2,520, which is seven times (7 × 360). Since this code work is universal it stands to reason it would work in North America as well for the Spanish explorers.

(29) This number means "expectancy" and the number 9 with it "judgment." It is tenth in the series of prime (indivisible) numbers and therefore partakes of the significance of 10.

(30) A most important number! This number is 3 times 10 (3

× 10 = 30) and denotes a high degree of perfection of the divine order, as marking the right moment. Jesus was in His 30th year when He began His ministry (Luke 3: 23). Thirty is traditionally a number signifying "completion", or the "end." In the Great Pyramid chronology, thirty is a Cycle of Renewal.

(31) The Hebrew expression of 31 is *El*, the name of God, and its signification, therefore, as a number or factor, would be "*deity*." It is 10 times the pi ratio (3.1416) and it is an important number in relation to the circle. The circle signifies "without beginning and ending" and the number 31 implies no beginning or ending. It is also eleventh in the series of prime (indivisible) numbers and partakes of the spiritual signification of the factor 11.

(37) The factor 37 is twelfth in the series of prime (indivisible) numbers; Therefore, it partakes of the significance of the number 12.

(38) Any time this number is found, whether it be in a row of rocks, dots on a cliff face or trees planted in a row it has a double significance. It is the number of "disobedience" because of the defection of God's people at Kadesh-Barnea (Deut. 1: 45 – 46; 2: 14 – 15). It is expectancy overshadowed by judgment, for it is 20 plus 9 doubled (20 + 9 + 9). On the other hand, for the faithful and obedient (Joshua and Caleb), it is the number of the shortened generation and a number that expresses consummation of expectancy. It marks the entry into "a land of promise," where a reward will be found. The secret number is 19.

(40) This was a very important number that occurs many times in the scriptures. It is associated with periods of probation, trial, and chastisement. Forty years is also applied as encompassing a generation (Num. 14: 34). Forty was used to denote the passing of a generation or a period of time.

(42) This number is identified with Antichrist (Rev. 13: 5). Another number associated with Antichrist is 1,260 (30 × 42). Its factors are 6 and 7 (6 × 7 = 42), indicating a connection between man and the Spirit of God, between Christ and Antichrist. Being a multiple of 7, it might be supposed that it would infer spiritual perfection, but in scriptural usage, this number is dominated by its association with 6, the number of man. Thus, 42 becomes significant of the working out of man's opposition to God. The background of the common phrase about everything being "at sixes and sevens" becomes obvious and, in this context, 42 is the number of *confusion*. It is also the number of "treading down" (Rev. 11: 2).

(43) The factor 43 is fourteenth in the series of prime (indivisible) numbers. Therefore, it partakes of the significance of the number 14. (See the meaning of 14). It is also one-tenth of 430 (see the meaning of 430).

(44) This number has special meanings and was used exclusively by Jesuits and other religious factions when referring to the "Consummation of the Age" as defined in the Great Pyramid, from the year 1909 to the year 1953 was 44 years. Therefore, 44 is the measure of consummation. It was also the number of years that Jacob's trouble was doubled (22 + 22 = 44): 22 years of physical suffering, laboring in a strange land for his wives, and 22 years of mental anguish in the loss of his son Joseph.

(47) The factor 47 is fifteenth in the series of prime (indivisible) numbers. Therefore, it partakes of the significance of the number 15.

(48) This number denotes government perfection, worldwide, because it is 4 times 12 (see the definitions of 4 and 12). It is also related to 144 (48 × 30), associating it with perfection in government and rule (see the definition of 144). It is the prophetic half hour (48 × 2 = 96).

(49) The Jubilee Count is 7 times 7, or 49 (7 × 7 = 49), at the end of which period, or its multiples, one year is added to obtain the fiftieth year—The Jubilee Year!

(50) This is the number of Jubilee or *deliverance*. It points to cessation and rest, following on as the result of the perfect consummation of time.

(51) This is an important number in chronology and Dr. E. W. Bullinger called it the number of "Divine Revelation." According to the Hebrew MSS (vernacular language) he maintained, the number of books in the Old Testament should be reckoned as 24: Ezra and Nehemiah reckoned as one book, with the one name, Ezra; each of the double books reckoned as one book (such as I & II Samuel, I & II Kings, I & II Chronicles); all the minor prophets reckoned as one book: The Book of the Minor Prophets. This would make 24 books in all (12 + 12 or 8 × 3), both sets of factors stamping the number with the seal of "Divine Perfection." With 27 books in the New Testament, the whole of the Divine Revelation contained in the Old and New Testaments (24 + 27 = 51), would be 51 books. Fifty-one is 17 times 3 (17 × 3 = 51) and therefore, very significantly, partakes of the spiritual attributes of the number 17.

(53) This number denotes the interval between signs, presaging the end. The great Star Shower occurred in 1833, which was 53 years after 1780, the year of the Dark Day!

(56) This is the perfect Lunar Cycle, the number of Aubrey Holes in the Aubrey Circle at Stonehenge, which is 288 feet (the number of Restoration) in diameter. The 56 Aubrey Holes served as a computer if you will. By using them to count the years, the Stonehenge priests could have kept accurate track of the moon and so could have predicted danger periods for the most spectacular eclipses of the moon and the sun. In fact, the Aubrey Circle could have been used to predict many celestial events. It is said of the Stonehenge priests that he who would track the moon would use a 56-year cycle. It will be recalled that the connotations of 7 and 8, in connection with 15 (7 + 8 = 15), introduce the perfect application of Divine Grace issuing in glory. That being true, the same connotations, by multiplication in connection with 56 (7 × 8 = 56), would greatly intensify the significance of both 7 and 8. In the Book of Revelation, the phrase, "I saw," occurs 56 times.

(58) This factor is 29 + 29 and signifies "Expectancy of Judgment Doubled."

(62) The 62 weeks of Daniel 9: 26 (2 × 31). This was the length of the ministry on earth of our Lord Jesus Christ. The number 62 was used to denote "*length of time*" spent by priests in obtaining spiritual blessings for the "Indians" in the southwest.

(65) This number is a multiple of 13 (13 × 5 = 65) and, in the scriptures it is especially associated with Ephraim, marking the apostasy of that tribe ("within threescore and five years shall Ephraim be broken, that it be not a people" —Isa. 7:88). The apostasy that began in Ephraim (Judges, chapter 17) afterward extended to the entire Ten Tribe Kingdom of the House of Israel, sometimes prophetically referred to as "Ephraim" or the "House of Joseph," of which Ephraim was a member, with Manasseh. Since the number of grace—5—enters into the computation (above), this is significant of the fact that Divine grace operates in behalf of God's people to bring them to a place of repentance and into compliance with His will.

(69) The 69 weeks of Daniel 9:25 (3 × 23). It is a factor related to *troubled times* and was used as a code number when the Spanish miners wished to convey that message to their comrades.

(70) This is a combination of two perfect numbers (7 × 10 = 70) and signifies "perfect spiritual order." We have seen something of the significance of their sum by addition in the number 17 (7 + 10 = 17); their product by multiplication is no less significant. It is the threescore and ten years of man's life (Ps. 90:10) and, without doubt, numbers the Jubilees from the organization of Israel into a Kingdom at Mount Sinai to the perfection of the Kingdom of God on earth, which is still future. Also, 70 is the number of Jerusalem and the number of *determination* (Dan. 9:24).

(75) This number is the difference between the prophetic numbers 1,260 and 1,335 given in the Book of Daniel (1,335 – 1,260 = 75). It is also the epact between 2,520 lunar and solar years.

(88) This number has the same significance, in progressively intensified from, that attaches to the series: 8:88:888. All indicate "resurrection," "renewal" or "divine intermediation."

(90) This number is one-half of the length of the Time of the End (180) and 28 × 90 = 2,520, or Seven Times. It is, therefore, one-fourth of a Time (360).

(96) This is a prophetic "day" (1/24th part of 2,304), 30 of which constitute a great "month" of 2,880, in either days or years. This number is the product of 8 times 12 (8 × 12 = 96) and combines the significances of both 8 and 12. It is one of the primary factors applied in the synchronization of time scales.

(99) This is the numerical value, in Greek, of the solemn "Amen" or "Verily" of our Lord Jesus Christ, summing up and ending His words. It is found on some ancient parchments.

(105) This is the Antediluvian Septinary Cycle (7 × 15 = 105.)

(113) This is the numerical value of *aish*, the Hebrew word for man.

(116) 116.26 pyramid inches. It is the length of the Antechamber in the Great Pyramid and the diameter of the year-circle whose circumference is 365.242 pyramid inches.

(120) This is the number of warning and first appears in the sixth chapter of Genesis in connection with the threatened judgment of the Deluge: "Consequently, the Ever-Living said, 'My spirit shall not call to man forever, for he is sinful flesh; but they shall have an hundred and twenty years'" (Gen. 6:3, Ferrar Fenton Trans.). It signifies, therefore, a divinely-appointed period of probation. Applied to persons, it points to a divinely-appointed number during a period of waiting (Acts 1:15). It is a factor when applied to the number of men who went up out of Egypt—that is, 600,000 (120 × 5000). It is also a factor in the great symbolic number 144,000 given in Revelations 14: 1, signifying those who stand with the Lamb on Mount Zion (120 × 1,200).

(126) This number means one-tenth (a tithe) of 1,260. It is also 3 × 42; 7 × 18; 6 × 21 (see definitions of all factors involved). It relates to the shortening of the days for the Elect's sake (Matt. 24:22).

(130) The number of the "appointed seed" (Gen. 4:25). Adam was 130 years old when Seth was born (Gen. 5:3).

(144) This number is very important and has always been to every dominating nation of the Old World. It was used widely and had serious meaning. This number has, as its primary factor, the number 12 (12 × 12 = 144), which associates it with perfection in government and rule. In the City of God there are 12 gates and 12 foundations; the city lies foursquare and the measure is 12,000 furlongs (Rev. 21:10 – 14). One hundred forty-four is the number of those who overcome and it is, of course, related to the 144,000, the symbolical whole number of those who will reign with Jesus Christ (Rev. 14: 1; 20:4). The number 10 signifies completion and when multiplied by 1,000, the Millennial number (100 × 100 = 1,000), the result (144 × 1,000 = 144,000) denotes the completion of His Body that makes up His entire staff of administrators who will be inducted into office to carry on the affairs of His Kingdom.

(153) This number is found in the final chapter of John's Gospel, in connection with the great take of fishes: "Simon Peter went up, and drew the net to land, full of great fishes, an hundred and fifty and three: and for all there were so many, yet was not the net broken" (John 21:11). One hundred fifty-three is, therefore, the number of the Elect since, at the commencement of His ministry, Jesus told two disciples: "I will make you fishers of men." This is a number that has taxed the ingenuity of some of the greatest Bible students from the earliest times, for all the possible mathematical combinations demonstrate it to be a factor of utmost significance. It is divided by 17 and is the sum of all numbers up to and including 17. There are 17 letters in the *Novus Ordo Seclorum* motto (meaning, "a new order of the ages") on the reverse side of the Great Seal of the United States and 153 is closely connected with United States history. The gematria of the expression, "sons of God," is exactly 153; therefore, it may be said that this is the number of the sons of God.

(178) In the Great Pyramid, the number 88 appears in the form of 2 times 88, plus 2 (178), this being the duration (on the inch-month scale) of the periods represented by the width of the walls of the Granite Coffer in the King's Chamber. Appearing both with and without addition of two days (the third day made perfect), the periods (2 × 88 = 176 or 2 × 88 = 178) bear the same connotations of divine intermediation as their undoubted factor (88).

(180) Time of the End! This designates the period of time when according to Daniel 12:4, "many shall run to and fro, and knowledge shall be increased." This number is one-half the cycle of 360 and is the epoch between the ending of 6,000 lunar years in AD 1821 and 6,000 solar years in AD 2001.

(200) This number stamps various things with insufficiency, even though 20 is the number of expectancy and here we have it tenfold (20 × 20 = 200). The implication is that something more is expected to achieve true completion. The significance of this number is suggested in the scriptures, where we read: "Two hundred pennyworth of bread is not sufficient to save him from the consequences of his sin (Joshua 7:21). This shows us the insufficiency of money. Absalom's 200 shekels weight of hair were not sufficient to save him but instead caused his destruction (II Sam. 14:26; 18:9-10). This shows us the insufficiency of beauty. Micah's graven image was purchased for 200 shekels (Judges 17:4) and led to idolatry. This shows us the insufficiency of mere religion. Ezra's 200 "singing men and singing women" (Ezra 2:65) were not sufficient to produce peace with God, true spiritual worship or joy in the Lord. This shows us the insufficiency of external things in the worship of God.

(217) The designed height of the Great Pyramid, without the Capstone, is 217 sacred or pyramid cubits. A line, at the angle of the Passage System, south of the east-west plane of the Great Pyramid, ends 217 miles at the true location of Mount Sinai.

(232) The designed height of the Great Pyramid, with the Capstone in place, is 232½ sacred or pyramid cubits. A line from the Capstone, projected at the Passage System angle, north of the east–west plane of the Great Pyramid, passes through the Sea of Reeds, where Israel crossed at the time of the Exodus, and ends 232½ geographic, or "perfect," miles, at Bethlehem.

(270) This number, the nine months of gestation or pregnancy, is given prophetic significance in the Second Book of Esdras in the Apocrypha: "As when a woman with child, in the ninth month, bringeth forth her son, within two or three hours of her birth, great pains compass her womb, which pains; they slack not a moment: even so shall not the plagues be slack to come upon the earth, and the world shall mourn, and sorrows shall come upon it on every side" (II Esdras 16:38-39). Thus, this number signifies *deliverance*, or the *birth of pangs* of a New World Order!

(285) This number is the common lunar cycle (19 × 15), proving the week has not been broken.

(286) This is truly a remarkable number, which is called the "Displacement Factor." When the Great Pyramid was built, an error of 286.1 (the actual mathematical value) in laying the base circuit made it impossible to place the headstone on the competed structure. Thus, in the Great Pyramid, this "displacement" error is symbolized in the fact that the entire passage system is 286.1 inches out of alignment by being east of the Great Pyramid's center plane. Not until the King's Chamber period is reached can one move westward to the true center of the structure. Therefore, 286, wherever applied in chronological reckoning, signifies man's displacement from God's plan of perfection. It is the measure of human error, warning that man and his plans and purposes are out of alignment with the divine will. When this displacement is overcome for the Building Race, as it will be, then the Headstone, or Chief Cornerstone—Jesus Christ—will take His rightful place in the "times of restitution of all things" (Acts 3:20-21), which will usher in the New Order of the Ages.

(315) This number is an accurate cycle, embracing, in one system, the movements of the sun and the moon.

(355) This number is the days in a lunar year.

(360) This is a most important number because it is the number of degrees in the ancient Hebrew day. One "Time" is 360, which is one-seventh of the great Seven Times (2,520 years). There is also the "prophetic year" of 360 days, 30 days of which constitute a "prophetic month." The mean (average) between the lunar year (355) and the solar year (365) is 360 days, the "prophetic year."

(365) This is the number of days in a solar year. It was the age of Enoch when he was translated.

(384) This factor is four "hours" or Watches, of 96 days, or years each.

(390) This number represents the period during which Ezekiel was told to bear the sins of Israel: "For I have laid upon thee the years of their iniquity, according to the number of the days, three hundred and ninety days so shalt thou bear the iniquity of the house of Israel" (Ez. 4-5). Therefore, this number applies particularly to the United States and Great Britain, as present-day Israel, and it signifies chastisement (13 × 30).

(391) This is the sum of the prophetic "hour, day, month and year" of Revelation 9:15.

(400) This is a divinely perfect period, the product of 8 times 50 (8 × 50 = 400). It is the number of years from the promise to

Abraham, at the birth of Isaac, to the Exodus (Gen. 15: 13). Stephen the Prophet mentions it as dating from "his seed" (Acts 7:6).

(420) This is the number of confusion (42), multiplied by 10 (42 × 10 =420), and indicates confusion coming to completion. It is one-sixth of the great Biblical Seven Times (420 × 6 = 2,520). Its basic significance, therefore, is that of *trial* or *judgment* upon the works of men.

(430) This is the number of years from the call of Abraham, or the promise made to him (Gen. 12:3) to the Exodus: "Now the sojourning of the children of Israel, who dwelt in Egypt, was four hundred and thirty years. And it came to pass at the end of the four hundred and thirty years, even the selfsame day it came to pass, that all the hosts of the Lord went out from the land of Egypt" (Ex. 12:40-41). It is the number of deliverance.

(434) This is the 62 weeks (62 × 7 = 434) given in Daniel 9: 25-27. It is the length, in days, of the ministry on earth of our Lord Jesus Christ.

(444) This is the numerical value of the name "Damascus," the oldest city of the Old World. It is the number of World Order.

(480) This is the temple number, being the number of years from the Exodus to the laying of the foundation of the first temple: "And it came to pass in the four hundred and eightieth year after the children of Israel were come out of the land of Egypt, in the fourth year of Solomon's reign over Israel, in the month *Zif*, which is the second month, that he began to build the house of the Lord" (1 Kings 6:1).

(490) This is the 70 weeks (70 × 7 = 490) mentioned in Daniel 9: 24. The Decree of Cyrus initiated the chronological reckoning that culminated in the anointing and baptism of Jesus on January 8, AD 28. It is a number signifying spiritual perfection.

(576) This number is the product of 38 (actually 38.4) times 15 (38.4 × 15 = 576) and represents an hour of consummated expectancy. It is one-half of 1,152, a number applied in the synchronization of time scales. Also, it is two times the number of restoration (2 × 288 = 576).

(630) This number is one quarter of the great Biblical Seven Times (630 × 4 = 2,520).

(666) This number is the number for *man* (Rev. 13:18). If 6 is the number of secular perfection, then 66 is a more emphatic expression of the same fact and 666 is the concentrated expression of it. This impressive number is, therefore, the trinity of human perfection, the "perfection of imperfection" through the culmination of human pride in independence of God and in opposition to Jesus Christ. In 1 Kings 10:14, this number also appears as the weight of gold that came to Solomon in one year. This associates the number with materialism, for basically it bears the stamp of human apostasy.

(840) This is the number of warning perfected (7 × 120 = 840), partaking of the perfect number 7 and the number of years of warning given to Noah concerning the Deluge. Used to denote impending disaster!

(880) This number exemplifies the various aspects of 88 since it is ten times that number (10 × 88 = 880). It partakes of its divine intermediation significance in intensified degree. In particular, this number points up developments that emphasize progression of the divine plan to lead wayward humanity back to righteousness through much tribulation.

(888) This grand number is the numerical value of the name "Jesus" in Greek. It is the superlative number of Jesus Christ.

(930) This factor (30 × 31) is the length of Adam's life. It is, therefore, the factor of the "Second [last] Adam" (see I Cor. 15:45; cf. Rom. 5:14).

(999) This is an intensified number of judgment, for it is the numerical value of the name "Sodom." It is also the numerical meaning of the phrase: "my wrath" (Heb. 3:8).

(1,000) This is the millennial number (Rev. 20:4). A day with the Lord is as a thousand years (II Peter 3: 8).

(1,040) This number is the difference between the prophetic numbers, 1,260 and 2,300 (1,260 + 1,040 = 2,300), which is both soli-lunar cycles. While this number does not appear on the surface of the Bible, it is used again and again in chronology. It signifies restoration and specifically defines the period during which plans or policies are brought to fruition; that is, to realization or accomplishment.

(1,081) Sometimes seen in Roman numeral form this number was used by early visitors to America. It can be found on rock panels in certain areas of the Southwest. This number is the number of the *abyss*, or the bottomless pit of the Book of Revelation; mostly used as a "danger" sign.

(1,152) This number is the length of a morning or the length of an evening, being one-half of 2,304. It was discovered that the length of time from the inception of the Korean War, on June 25, 1950, to the termination of the Consummation of the Age, on August 20, 1953, was 1,152 days, establishing its importance as a chronological time measure. There are seven periods of 1,152 days from June 25, 1950 to the top of the King's Chamber in the Great Pyramid on July 23, 1972 (six periods of 1,152 days from August 20, 1953 to the top of the King's Chamber on July 23, 1972). Factors in computations of its division are 96, 144, 286, 288 and 576 (importantly, 12 × 96 = 1,152).

(1,222) This is the number of solar years in 1,260 lunar years.

(1,260) This is the number of "Trials and Tribulations." It appears several times in the Bible in various forms. It is mentioned twice in the twelfth chapter of Revelation in connection with the "woman" in the "wilderness." In verse 6 the period is given as "a thousand, two hundred and threescore days," while, in verse 14, it is written: "a time (360), and times (2 × 360 = 720), and half a time (180)." Since a Biblical "time" is 360, three and a half "times" would be 1,260. Twice in the Book of Revelation the period is given as "forty and two months" (Rev. 11:2 & 13:5). The "prophetic month" contains 30 days (42 × 30 = 1,260). The period appears twice in the Book of Daniel; once as "a time, and times, and the dividing of time" and once as "a time, times, and an half" (Dan. 7:25 & 12:7). It is also found in Revelation 11: 3, "And I will give power unto my two witnesses, and they shall prophesy a thousand two hundred and threescore days, clothed in sackcloth." It is one-half of Seven Times (360 + 2 × 360 + 180 =1,260; 7 × 360 = 2,520).

(1,290) This is the number of desolation and the desolator, taken from the final chapter of the Book of Daniel.

(1,335) This is the number of blessing or blessedness, taken from the final chapter of the Book of Daniel: "Blessed is he that waiteth and cometh to the thousand three hundred and five and thirty five days" (Dan. 12:11). This number frequently has a dual significance: *blessing* upon God's people, charged with the responsibility to restore the administration of the Law of the Lord as the law of their land, and *judgment* upon those nations and peoples who set themselves in opposition to God and His people.

(1,493) In Matthew 25:6 we read: "At midnight there was a cry made." In the Greek text the expression, "At midnight," has the numerical value of 153 + 300 + 1,040, or 1,493. The Greek expression does not necessarily mean absolute midnight, but rather "in the middle of the night." This number was used as a coded symbol.

(1,600) This number is the length of the Battle Line and is found in the final book of the Bible: "And the winepress was trodden without the city, and blood came out of the winepress, even unto the horses bridles, by the space of a thousand and six hundred furlongs" (Rev. 14:20). It is a number specifically associated with Divine Judgment, marking events as divine pressures are applied to faulty institutions and procedures of materialistic humanity. Any development which serves to intensify the ordeal of world judgment may be marked by this factor.

(1,890) This number denotes travail perfected. It partakes of the significance of the number of gestation (9 × 30 = 270) in intensified form because it is 7 times that number (7 × 270 = 1890).

(2,300) This is the number that measures the period during which the Holy Army of God is to be trodden down prior to the cleansing of the sanctuary: "How long shall be the vision concerning the daily sacrifice, and the transgression of desolation, to give both the sanctuary and the host to be trodden under foot? And he said unto me, unto two thousand and three hundred days; then shall the sanctuary be cleansed" (Dan. 8:13-14). This number marks activities of the nations of Israel as they contend with tyrannous usurpation and aggression. It applies to various way marks on the road to world cleansing through extreme tribulation.

(2,340) This number is the length of a morning and evening, taken from the answer of "that certain saint" who was *Palmoni*, the Numberer of Secrets or Wonderful Numberer. It is a measure used in the synchronization of time scales with Great Pyramid chronology. There are just three days, comprising 2,304 mornings and evenings, from August 20, 1953 to the top of the King's Chamber on July 23, 1972.

(2,520) This is the Great Seven Times of Prophecy, the divinely ordained number setting the duration of disciplinary punishment. It is mentioned recurrently in the 26th chapter of Leviticus where the people of Israel were given their choice between blessings for obedience to the Law of God or punishment for flouting it: "And if ye will not yet, for all this, hearken unto me, then I will punish you seven times more for your sins" (Lev. 26:18; also verses 21 & 24). It is a number expressive of chronological perfections, being seven times the Biblical year of 360 days (7 × 360 = 2,520). It is the product of four numbers of completion or perfection (3 × 7 × 10 × 12 = 2,520). It is the Least Common Multiple (LCM) of all the ten numbers from which our system of notation is derived (the LMC of 1, 2, 3, 4, 5, 6, 7, 8, 9, 10 is 2,520).

(4,313) This number has the Greek value meaning: "Sign of the son of Man."

(5,040) This number is not mentioned in the Bible but it lies at the basis of an ancient Biblical system of chronological prophecy. It is not only divisible by 7 and by 70 and by 315, the accurate cycle that embraces, in one system, the movements of the sun and moon, but also by 360 (a Time), and by 1,260, as well as by 2,520 without remainder. Plato refers to the importance of this number.

(5,820) This is the number of solar years in a lunar period of 6,000 years.

(6,000) This is the working week of six days of 1,000 years each, at the end of which the Millennium of Rest will come.

(7,000) This is the entire week of human history, being seven days of 1,000 years each. Its final "day" of 1,000 years is designated in the book of Revelations as the Millennium of Rest and it will be the period of the reign of righteousness when "the earth shall be filled with the knowledge of the glory of the Lord, as the waters cover the sea" (Hab. 2:14).

(144,000) Here we end our language of numbers with this number of superlative significance. In the first place, 12 signifies perfection in government and 144, the number of the rulers, or those who overcome, is 12 times 12 (12 × 12 = 144). Secondly, 10 denotes both completion and perfection and its multiplication by 100, to produce the product of 1,000 (100 × 10 = 1,000) suggests the combining of all the meanings, intensified manifold, of its factors. Therefore, the whole sum (144 × 1,000 = 144,000) denotes the completion and perfection of the divine government, being the symbolical number designating the completed roster of those who will "live and reign with Christ a thousand years" (Rev. 20:4, 6).[1]

NOTES

1. Courtesy in part by Destiny Publishers, Merrimac, Massachusetts.

BIBLIOGRAPHY

Fell, Barry. *America B.C.* New York: Pocket Books, 1976.

Hall, Stan. *Tayos Gold.* Kempton: Adventures Unlimited Press, 2006.

Hansen, L. Taylor. *He Walked the Americas.* Amherst: Legend Press, 1963.

Jenkins, Timothy R. *The Ten Tribes of Israel.* Ancient American Foundation, 2005.

Little, Gregory, Lora Little, and John Van Auken. *Mound Builders.* Memphis: Eagle Wing Books Inc., 2001.

May, Wayne. *This Land: Zarahemla and the Nephite Nation.* Colfax: Ancient American Archaeology, 2002.

Martineau, LaVan. *The Rocks Begin to Speak.* Las Vegas: KC Publications, 1973.

Mertz, Henrietta. *The Mystic Symbol.* Global Books, 1986.

Porter, Bruce, Rod Meldrum. *Prophecies Promises.* Digital Legend, 2009.

Priest, Josiah. *American Antiquities and Discoveries in the West.* Albany: Hoffman & White, 1834.

Rydholm, C. Fred. *Michigan Copper, The Untold Story*. Tok: Winter Cabin Books, 2006.

Rydholm, C. Fred, Russell E. Burrows. *The Mystery Cave of Many Faces*. Marquette: Superior Heartland, 1992.

Shaffer, Steve. "The Aagard Lamp." *Ancient American Magazine*. Vol 13. Issue 84. 2010.

Smith, Ethan. *View of the Hebrews*. ed. Charles D. Tate Jr., 2nd ed. Provo: BYU Religious Studies Center, 1996.

Squier, E.G. *Antiquities of New York*. Buffalo: G.H. Derby, 1850.

Wingate, Richard. *Atlantis in the Amazon: Lost Technologies and the Secrets of the Crespi Treasure*. Rochester: Bear & Company, 2011.

Wolter, Scott F. *The Hooked X*. Self published, 2009.

ABOUT THE AUTHOR

Steve Shaffer was born in Salt Lake City, Utah, August 12, 1947. He is married to Bonnie Peay and together they have ten children.

Steve has spent a great deal of his life in the mountains and deserts of the west in an attempt to trace the steps of the ancient inhabitants that once roamed the land.

His education spans several decades. He has a bachelor of science degree a master of arts degree and a graduation diploma from the North American School of Conservation. He has authored several books including sections on Spanish symbols documentation and ancient symbols identification. Shaffer is considered by most as the expert in Spanish symbols identification. He also was instrumental in the transliteration of the Chalk Creek hieroglyphic panel east of Fillmore, Utah. He has appeared in several documentaries such as *Tops of the Mountains, an Illustrated History of Utah*; *National Geographic EXPLORER; The Secret History of Gold;* and others now pending release. He has lectured extensively and is sought after by many groups for his knowledge in his field of expertise.

Steve is the President of "The We Nooch Society" a historical preservation society based out of Santaquin, Utah. Visit www.wenooch.org for more information.

He is also a Vietnam War veteran serving in combat with the 2/16 Inf. Rangers in 1967–68.

0 26575 10223 9